THE ENCYCLOPEDIA OF
FLOWER
ARRANGING

THE ENCYCLOPEDIA OF
FLOWER
ARRANGING

Susie Edwards

SMITHMARK

© Salamander Books Ltd 1997

This edition published in 1997 by
SMITHMARK publishers,
a division of U.S. Media Holdings, Inc.,
16 East 32nd Street,
New York, NY 10016

9 8 7 6 5 4 3 2 1

SMITHMARK books are available for bulk purchase for sales promotion and premium use. For details, write or call the manager of special sales,
SMITHMARK Publishers
16 East 32nd Street, New York,
NY 10016; (212) 532-6600

ISBN 0-7651-9939-4

CREDITS
Commissioning Editor: Alice Duke
Project Editor: Joanna Smith
Designer: Paul Johnson
Color Reproduction: The Emirates
  Press, Dubai
Printed and bound in China

CONTENTS

BEFORE YOU BEGIN

~

THE MOTIVATION FOR arranging flowers is as varied as the plant materials we choose. The common thread is the desire to produce something pleasing to the eye, decorative and suited to its situation. The old adage 'beauty is in the eye of the beholder' holds true here. Your favourite flower may be totally unappealing to someone else. When you choose which to use, pick those which appeal to you. You will feel more comfortable working with materials you already find stimulating before you begin.

It will depend on how fanatical you are about the art of flower arranging – and it is an art – just how much time and effort (and money) you wish to spend on it. Above all, you must enjoy what you do. The older I get the more convinced I am that the medium of plant material is not so different from paint or even thread. Concern about your skills, the quality or condition of the flowers or a bad mood before you start, will influence the way you handle your materials and the finished result. Relax and get in tune with the beautiful things you have to work with and you will make the best out of your flowers.

Flower arranging can also be great therapy. Approached the right way it can be both relaxing and satisfying. It should be enjoyable and fun, otherwise why bother? Worldwide, thousands of us bother, in a great variety of styles, so it can't be that terrifying or difficult. Begin with something simple and progress to the more advanced once you have learned some of the techniques.

With such a simple glass container, you can afford to be daring
with the colour scheme. Early autumn presents a luscious selection
of combinations to try.

THE PRINCIPLES OF FLOWER ARRANGING

Good use of these very fundamental parts of design is as important in flower arranging as in any other form of art. They are the following:

Balance – both physical and visual are just as important. Colour, texture and line all play their part in achieving a stable design.

Scale – this is the relationship a component has with other components as well as the container.

Proportion – very closely related to Scale but it refers to the relationship between the components with regard to quantity.

Rhythm – can be found with the use of line, pattern and colour leading the eye through and in and out of the design. An arrangement without rhythm is static and easily boring.

Contrast – this is achieved by placing differing textures and forms against each other and goes a long way to producing Harmony.

Harmony – this results in a relaxed and comfortable feel to a design.

Below: The starting point of flowering arranging: a classic border, a joy to behold. Although the grass is showing signs of stress from water shortage, the flowers are revelling in the summer sun.

Dominance – is linked to Proportion. An example is the focal point of a design, towards the centre, where massing or the use of colour emphasises that area. Quantity, size, colour, form and texture all relate to this principle. Too little produces a bland, boring design but too much is overkill and ruins the relationship between the principles.

By using these principles with care to begin with, they easily become second nature as you become familiar with the techniques of arrangement.

Above: The finishing point of flower arranging: a simple but beautiful posy design with a perfect balance of textures and form.

THE ELEMENTS OF DESIGN

The senses are all important in every aspect of our lives. In flower arranging, the visual perception of the materials used is paramount to a proper understanding of this highly creative activity.

Form

It is easy to see the shape of an individual piece of plant material. This is known as form. Linear materials are useful in creating outlines, as are flatter branches, while rounded or 'blobby' shapes provide the important features or points of interest. In between these two the areas to be filled need fussier, lighter materials and these are called transitional shapes. Without these variations, a design easily loses vitality and that special attraction over another. The use of these shapes within a design making flowing, curving or even straight lines produces movement within that design. A flat, static arrangement is such a waste of beautiful flowers and leaves, and thus 'line' puts rhythm and interest in and helps to make the best of your chosen materials.

Colour

This is a very emotive element. Colour affects each one of us differently. Magenta may do wonders for one person while it positively upsets another! Colours create different moods and their appearance differs according to the amount of light available, the texture of the subject and also from how far away it is viewed. I will go into more detail in the section on Colour Theory which is on page 14.

Texture

The appearance of a leaf, petal or stem, whether it is rough, smooth,

Right: Four examples of different forms. The statuesque form of the Artichoke's flower spikes and cut leaves (top left) are wonderfully architectural. The fuzzy leaves of Fennel (top right) make a soft, rounded outline; this is also an example of a fussy texture. Hosta leaves (bottom left) have very bold, curved forms; while Sunflowers (bottom right) have rounded forms with happy faces.

Right: Four examples of different textures. The bark (top left) has a strong, spaced texture where colour also plays a part in the pattern; while the bark (top right) has craggy clefts which again produce a strong feel. The carpet of Soleirolia, *or* Helxine *(bottom left) is a good example of a fine texture.* Cotinus, *the Smoke Bush, (bottom right) is a lovely fuzzy texture.*

hairy or shiny is a very tangible element. Contrasting textures give different materials the ability to show themselves to best advantage. Experiment: take two pieces of plant material such as *Pittosporum* and Privet. That may be all you have in the way of foliage. They are similar in leaf size and the overall pattern they make and, when close together, they become muddled and ineffective. Now take a third item, such as a *Bergenia, Hosta* or even large Ivy leaf and tuck between the two first stems. They will instantly take on their own identity and character and become three distinct areas of texture. The change of form here also plays an important role. I think this has to be my favourite element if it is possible to say such a thing, because for me this puts the 'feel' into things and then involves another of the senses – touch. Flower arranging is considered a visual art and yet I am sure potters and sculptors will agree that there is a positive pleasure from handling the materials with which we work. To

stroke the velvety surface of a *Stachys byzantina* leaf or feel the craggy strength of a piece of driftwood or bark are sensations which must influence the work produced with those materials.

Space
Space within a design always helps to define the shapes of the component parts. Designs in a more traditional style make use of smaller areas of space while more modern pieces often use space as a component itself. The spaces around stems and flowers allow each to play its full part and without them designs become compacted, heavy and static. An arrangement should also be in scale with the space it occupies whether in the home or in a competition.

At times I find it difficult to separate the elements from each other as they are so interconnected. Careful attention to the four, in addition to the principles, makes for good grounding in the theory behind the skill.

CHOOSING CONTAINERS

There are so many things to consider when choosing a container for an arrangement. It must obviously be suited to the style of the room in which it is to go as well as to the type of display you are going to put in it. Is it to be an all-round design or just to face front? Is it to be placed low down, table height or above eye level? And is the material from which it is made sympathetic to the design you are planning?

The more formal the design the more formal the container should be. A basket can be quite sophisticated when the flowers in it are arranged in a controlled fashion, but with a looser design with garden plant material it can become wonderfully rustic. Glassware is in abundance these days with new and exciting shapes in every shop and these new shapes provide great opportunities for the arranger, but there are plenty of traditional glass vases too. A Victorian glass epergne would not be a comfortable choice for a very modern flat but would so easily set the scene as a table centre for a tiny Victorian terraced house. As with so many aspects of flower arranging, experimentation is the answer to a lot of decisions regarding containers and favourites will emerge.

Some containers are just that and not really meant to be seen – the small plastic saucers for foam, for instance. An effort should be made to make this type less obvious once the flowers are arranged. Containers which have a function in their own right, on the other hand, such as jugs, baskets and lidded boxes, look best if it is still

obvious what the container was before the flowers were added. It is therefore better in these cases to allow the container to play an important part in the design. Here, therefore, the colour, form and texture of the container are just as important as they are for the plant material. It is worth remembering that white is the most obvious of colours and catches the eye and holds it. If you wish to use a white container, always try to add white flowers to the arrangement too, so that the eye does not linger for too long on the container and hence the base of the design.

Making the choice as to which container to use for an arrangement is still very much down to personal preference in the end. The container should be practical and hold sufficient water or foam to give the flowers a continual source of water without constant topping up. The choice of mechanics may have a bearing on the container you use too. Some will need a liner if you are using wire netting, to eliminate any damage to the container. Although many new baskets are lined with polythene, take care you do not puncture this lining and endeavour to find a different sort of liner for a more permanent solution.

Remember that with a little ingenuity and thought, you could use anything from an old boot to a bucket or an egg cup to an urn for putting your flowers in. Always bear in mind the scale and proportion of the container when making your choice, and the more simple the line of the container, the easier it will be to get the best from your design.

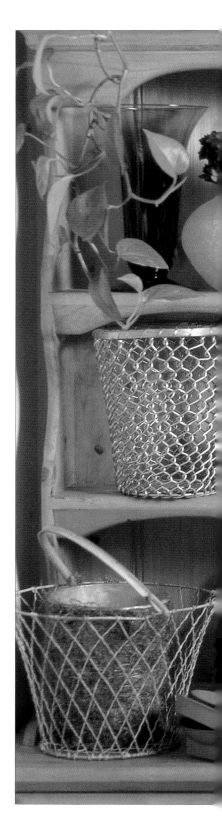

Below: From wire to wood, from glass to brass and everything in between. Collect a good cross-section of styles and categories of container, bearing in mind your home environment.

COLOUR THEORY

Being surrounded with different colours everywhere, we often take them for granted. Imagine how strange it would feel if the whole world was only blue or only yellow. As individuals, we often favour one colour over another, some of us to excess. The changes of fashionable colours in clothes and so on each year move us constantly on, and, as it is easy to tire of one colour or combination of colours, the move regularly refreshes the eye and its perception of colour. Fundamentally, colour is a very personal thing, some people preferring soft pastels, some bright primary colours and others the more muted variations and neutral colours. If we all liked the same things the world would be a very different place.

Whatever your preferences, though, it is necessary to understand a little of how colour functions, in order to use it well within your flower arrangements. Pure colours excite the eye easily but tire it quickly, so use them in moderation except where you need to make a vivid statement. Tints, tones and shades (which are pure colours with the addition of white, grey or black respectively) are much easier to live with. Flowers are such transient things, though, and bright colours begin to fade so quickly that for the home they are probably not there long enough to become very obtrusive. In the scheme of things a flower arrangement is quite small, and so a design of bright clear colours will be stimulating and eye catching, but too many designs of this nature in a small area will be overpowering and far less acceptable.

Always remember that the warm colours – oranges and reds – appear to advance in a design. Blues and greens are considered cool colours; blue recedes while green stays neutral in movement. All colours affect each other, but yellow and violet are particularly influenced by those nearby. They can be warm or cool, and thus advance or recede, according to which colours are around them. In practical terms, it means that care should be taken when using a colour such as purple towards the centre of a design as it can easily become a black hole. In this instance, it is also to do with the absorption of light. The direction and quantity of light play a large part in changing the appearance of a colour – dark colours absorb light and light colours reflect it.

Tints, tones and shades (colours which have been modified by adding black or white or grey) become wonderfully soft and subtle and these are the colours which are an advantage when used for containers, backgrounds or accessories used with arrangements. White added to different colours makes them more visible. White is also the lightest colour visually, followed by yellow, through to the heaviest violet and then black. White, black and grey are considered to be neutral colours. White added to a colour produces a tint, black a shade and grey a tone.

Colours can affect the mood of an arrangement, too, and in turn the mood of the viewer. The warmer colours add warmth, gaiety and vibrancy and the cool ones coolness, calm, and even melancholy. Carefully chosen, a particular colour can subtly create just the right atmosphere in a room for a specific occasion. Tradition and symbolism often involve colour choices too. So, when choosing a colour scheme, take into account the background and the surroundings and possibly the psychological effect required. Using white and green for a meal on a hot summer day will cool your guests, while a combination of clashing reds will warmly welcome visitors who have ventured out in freezing winter conditions.

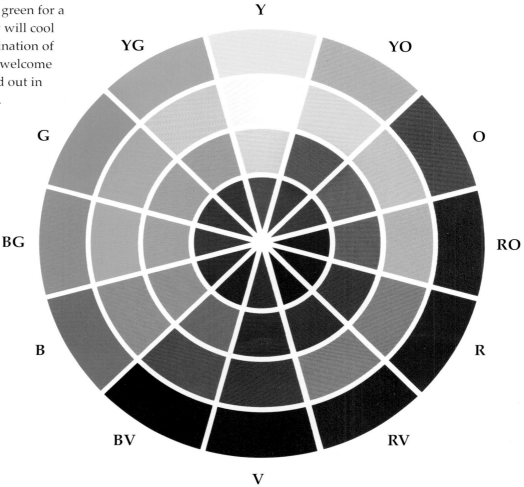

The Colour Wheel

The colour wheel (above) is a device used to help explain colour theory and is a useful tool for evaluating and planning arrangements.

The outer band of the colour wheel is made up of the three primary colours: yellow, red and blue. When pairs of primary colours are mixed, the secondary colours are formed: orange, violet and green. When each of the secondary colours is mixed with the adjacent primary colours, the tertiary colours are made: yellow-

orange, red-orange, red-violet, blue-violet, blue-green and yellow-green.

The outer band of the colour wheel is made up of the pure colours. The second band is made up of the tints, which are the pure colours but each with white added. The third band is the tones, pure colours with grey added, while the inner band is the shades, pure colours with black added. There are an infinite number of tints, tones and shades, made by adding different amounts of white, grey or black, but only one of each is shown.

Key to Colour Wheel

Y	*yellow*
YO	*yellow-orange*
O	*orange*
RO	*red-orange*
R	*red*
RV	*red-violet*
V	*violet*
BV	*blue-violet*
B	*blue*
BG	*blue-green*
G	*green*
YG	*yellow-green*

COLOUR THEORY IN PRACTICE

It is better to learn the basic colour schemes open to flower arrangers before you experiment. They are:

Monochromatic schemes – these use the tints, tones and shades of any one colour, effectively any of the segments of the colour wheel, such as the red segment or the blue-green segment.

Adjacent schemes – these use the colours lying next to each other in the colour wheel, that is any three or five adjacent segments, such as blue, blue-violet and violet; or yellow-green, yellow and yellow-orange.

Complementary schemes – these make use of colours which lie opposite or nearly so on the colour wheel, such as orange and blue; or yellow and violet.

Triadic schemes – these schemes use three colours equidistant on the wheel, such as yellow, blue and red; or violet, orange and green.

Polychromatic schemes – a mixture of many colours, taken from anywhere on the colour wheel.

On first reading this, it may appear that colour theory is complicated, but don't be put off. So much of it just comes naturally so follow your instincts to begin with. With practice, you will soon see where one

A monochromatic scheme: a complete range of tints, tones and shades of yellow from the pure colour (seen in the Achillea) *to soft pastels and almost khaki. All the colours are found in the yellow segment of the colour wheel.*

An adjacent scheme: here from yellow to the next segments in the colour wheel of yellow-green and green on the one side and yellow-orange on the other. This could have included a stronger orange too, and still have been within the classification of an adjacent scheme.

particular colour used in recession is
more effective than another, or where
another dominates a design to its
detriment. Keep checking the few
guidelines above as you learn to
arrange and it will soon become an
automatic process to evaluate the
colours being used. Extra care should
be taken when producing work for a
competition, though, particularly if
colour features in the class title.

*Right: An adjacent colour scheme
using red, red-violet, violet and
blue-violet and the tints, tones and
shades of those colours.*

*A complementary scheme: yellow is
directly opposite to violet on the colour
wheel and this combination produces a
very striking and dramatic example of
this type of colour scheme.*

*A triadic scheme: red, yellow and blue,
the three primary colours, are the classic
mixture for a representation of triadic
colour. It tends to produce a rather brash
effect but is nevertheless useful at times.
This is a combination which appeals to
children but is one which is tiring to the
eye in large doses. It is important here to
include the tints, tones and shades of each
colour to alleviate the effect of too much
pure colour.*

17

STYLE AND SHAPE

BASIC POSY DISPLAY USING FOAM

The making of a posy arrangement is one of the fundamental techniques of flower arranging, the equivalent of learning to make a roux in cookery. This one is in floral foam. Learn the method first and then make it smaller or larger as the occasion arises. You can use this technique with any fresh or dried material.

Step 1

Cut a piece of foam to fit the container, soak in water to wet it right through, and tape into the bowl with anchor tape. Make sure the foam stands proud of the top of the container. Leave spaces around the square piece of foam as this makes it easier to keep topping up the reservoir with water to ensure the foam never dries out. In this case, the bowl was about 8in (20cm) across and just under half a standard block of foam fitted neatly inside it.

Step 2

Cut small pieces of foliage, such as Euonymus, *about 5in (12.5cm) long. Place one stem almost vertically in the centre and insert more, radiating them towards the centre around the edge of the bowl. Make sure these initial pieces go in close to the edge of the bowl. They will be almost horizontal. Then add more foliage to fill in between, increasing the steepness of the angle of insertion but still radiating the pieces from the centre.*

Step 3

Intersperse with another variety of material to make a dome-shaped skeleton of foliage. I have used small stems of Skimmia *leaves with flowers. Continually turn the container round as you work to avoid achieving a two-sided design and not the all-round arrangement you want.*

Step 4

Begin over again with flowers such as Freesia, *putting in radiating stems and height in the same way as you used the* Euonymus. *Place three* Nerine *around the edge, making sure to keep within the dome shape, but altering the angle they enter the foam so you avoid making a frill. Use two more* Nerine *at different heights in the top part of the arrangement.*

Step 5

Add some larger flowers, such as Roses (still keeping within the dome shape) distributing them evenly through the arrangement. Some can be a little shorter to help bring depth into the design. Tuck in a few pieces of conifer foliage to fill in any gaps where you can still see foam. If you attempt this design on a larger scale, you will need to sink more flowers deeper in amongst the rest to avoid an almost two-dimensional effect.

BASIC POSY DISPLAY USING WIRE

This version of the posy is made with wire netting as the means of support. In the end, whether you use foam or wire is probably your personal preference. Wire netting produces a much looser, more relaxed feel. Where there is danger of water spillage, foam may be the better choice of mechanics, but you will have to work harder to produce the lightness of flowers arranged in wire.

When I was taught flower arranging, I was told to turn my first arrangement in wire netting upside down! The only thing that was supposed to fall out was the water. It does work if you have the correct combination of wire density and quantity of flowers. Do try it; it is an amazing boost to your morale when it works and it does make you try to secure the stems better in the first place.

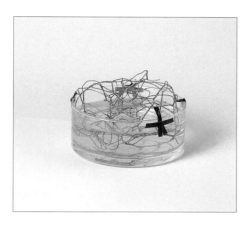

Step One

Crumple the wire netting into a loose ball and fit into the container. Take note of the density of wire in the illustration and try to achieve the same effect. You will soon find out if you have too much or too little once you begin to arrange, so it is better to start again with a new piece right at the beginning if necessary. If the container you choose is glass, use tape to fix the wire in place, sticking the tape close to the rim of the bowl so it will be easy to hide. With ceramic containers, it is best to hold the netting in place using reel wire, wrapping it around the container very much as you would use string to tie up a parcel. Make sure the wire is linked on the underside to enable you to pull it tight. Twist the ends together to secure it firmly.

Step Two

When the wire is securely in place, fill the container with water. Begin placing small lengths of foliage (here Viburnum tinus*) around the rim of the container radiating from a central point, threading them through the netting. Keep turning the arrangement round all the time. Place other small pieces more vertically in the centre. Don't worry if the original pieces move when you add more. They will for a while until there is sufficient material in the netting for the stems to properly intertwine and hold together. Make a small, round domed outline of foliage. Add three big Ivy leaves at slightly different angles tucked in between the other foliage. Try to avoid placing them horizontally as it produces a kind of frill effect.*

Step Three

Next start adding some flowers. Trim the stems (here Nigella*) and remove most of the small buds to avoid making the whole thing too fussy. Keeping within the shape of the foliage, add the* Nigella *filling in the dome shape but keeping it light and airy. Other flowers, such as Roses, can then be interspersed equally around the shape already defined by the foliage and by the* Nigella.

Step Four

Cut some yellow Centaurea *a bit shorter than the other flowers, and recess them into the arrangement to take the eye deeper in. If you have remembered to keep turning the arrangement as you work, it will be easy to get an equal distribution of flowers. I cannot emphasise enough how important it is to turn it; it may be a help to use a small turn-table. It is not essential but I find them useful; however, I do know arrangers who hate them. Finally, pop in some white Chincherinchee (*Ornithogalum*) at a length somewhere between the Roses and the* Centaurea.

BASIC FACING DISPLAY USING FOAM

This is a facing arrangement which has the outer quarters filled in well to ensure that side views are as effective as the front. It is important to place some of the side stems facing to the back as well, to give the whole design depth. Without this, the arrangement is easily unbalanced and looks as though it is an all-round arrangement which has been cut in half. It is similar to an all-round arrangement, but because the main vertical stem is not centrally placed, there is less material in the back section than the front and the sides. This particular facing display is arranged in floral foam which helps to add a smart, formal appearance to the design.

Step One

Soak a block of foam and cut it to fit in the container. Leave spaces each side as these facilitate topping up with water. Chamfer the edges of the foam. In this example, the foam was such a tight fit and the arrangement was not big or heavy, so it was not necessary to secure the foam further with anchor tape. However, if your efforts to cut the foam to size leave it fitting loosely, it would be sensible to wrap it round with tape, ensuring that it goes all the way round and sticks back onto itself as it is more adhesive to itself than to anything else. Arrange the container so that the tape wraps around it from side to side rather than back to front so it will be easier to disguise.

Step Two

Cut stems of foliage, such as Beech, at an acute angle and make a gently domed shape with them in the foam. First insert a central vertical stem approximately three quarters of the way back and then radiate horizontal stems from a point within the container and on the central line. Place some shorter stems leading backwards to help create extra depth, and also balance the arrangement by giving extra visual weight at the base. I have done this by adding two Bergenia leaves, placed close together, in the front over the rim of the container, to make one area of texture rather than splitting their placement. Two items make the eye jump from one to the other in a straight line. By making one group, the leaves begin to add focal interest. The pattern made by the repeated curved edges also creates interest.

Step Three

Keeping within the outline of foliage, place some erect flowers, such as Celosia and Stocks, around the edges, again repeating the backward movement with a couple of the lower placed stems. Place one of the stems of Stock coming forwards from the middle, but make sure that it is not left too long making a bulbous shape from a side view. This would give the arrangement an overblown and overbalanced look even when viewed from the front.

Step Four

Fill in the central area with Cirsium and Cosmos flowers, using the largest and most open flowers towards the centre and lower down in the design. These flowers will be slightly shorter than the outline material. Then tuck in even shorter pieces of Limonium to occupy the spaces between. Check for any gaps and add small pieces of foliage to cover any exposed foam if necessary. Make sure that there are sufficient flowers in the side areas and also flowing backwards to create a deep arrangement. Imagine looking down from above the design: only a small wedge at the back of the display should be left without flowers, although this should be tidied with foliage at the very end.

BASIC FACING DISPLAY USING WIRE

This informal, loose facing design is an effect which is much more easily achieved with wire netting as a means of support, than with foam. Foam gives a more formal effect. Garden flowers and foliage lend themselves to this type of arrangement, but during the summer months it is possible to buy such material from a florist's shop. If the *Hosta* leaves prove a problem, try cutting a few leaves from a suitable houseplant instead.

Step One

Firstly crumple wire netting into a suitable shape for the container, in this case an ovoid. Tie the netting securely in place with reel wire as described in the posy design on page 21. Remember not to begin any arrangement until the mechanics are rock solid. Fill the container with water. Establish the required height, approximately twice the height of the container, with a straight branch of foliage such as Pittosporum, *placing it on a centre line but about three-quarters of the way back in the container. Add branches to each side threading them through the netting and radiating them from the centre stem.*

Step Two

Add more foliage – I have used Senecio greyii *and* S. cineraria *– flowing over the front rim and spreading backwards too, creating extra depth in the arrangement. Without this depth, a facing arrangement can look like an all-round design cut in half, and appears stiff and unbalanced. In effect, the stems placed to define the width and depth are placed almost completely round the rim. Those at the front are shorter than those at the sides and those towards the back should be lifted a bit higher. The outline should be a gentle rounded arch. Three* Hosta *leaves are positioned to create a focal area and the beautiful glaucous blue Rue placed centrally is a marvellous change of texture ensuring the best is made of both* Hosta *and* Rue.

Step Three

The bunch of Delphinium *contained one pink-mauve stem which was left out to avoid ruining the colour scheme. Therefore, two* Delphinium *stems are placed in the top of the arrangement close together to make one splash of blue, while the other two are to the side and the front, keeping within the shape made by the foliage, making three areas of blue only. Four stems placed separately would have made a square shape within the arrangement. The eye tends to rest on each corner in turn and not absorb the rest of the design. Note they are not placed equally to each side; this keeps the informality and does not make a stiff triangle. Some stems of white Stock are cut slightly shorter and placed between the* Delphinium.

Step Four

The spikes of white Primulinus Gladioli contrast well arranged between the softer forms of Stock and Delphinium *and the foliage, as do the round forms of blue Echinops. Three large yellow garden Roses complete the arrangement, added rather casually. The centre one attracts the eye to the middle of the design and keeps drawing it back as it takes in the rest of the arrangement.*

BASIC PEDESTAL DISPLAY

A pedestal arrangement is similar in construction to a facing design; remember that everything must radiate from that central line about three quarters of the way back in the piece of foam. Taking into account the height of the stand, the arrangement should be approximately one and a half to two times its width. That is the measurement from the bottom of the trailing pieces to the top of the central backing stem. In this particular pedestal arrangement, a tall slim plant stand makes an elegant support for a collection of wonderfully full summer flowers and foliage. Trails of Bryony and tassels of *Amaranthus* reinforce the relaxed feel, and beautiful blown garden Roses and Peonies look soft and epitomise the season.

Step One

Soak the foam, chamfer the edges, place in a saucer and cover with wire netting. Attach and secure the wire using reel wire as described on page 21. Evaluate the materials you have collected together and choose those branches which naturally fall, to use for the sides and edges so that the appearance is a very natural one. Choosing less floppy stems will create a gently rounded off triangular background with an undulating edge. As with the facing design, make sure some materials flow backwards too. Very traily pieces such as Bryony or Ivy are best added at this stage as it is difficult to get them in later.

Step Two

Add further pieces of foliage and place two strong leaves, such as Hosta, overlapping each other to the front of the saucer. Place some erect flowers like Antirrhinum around the edges, about the same length as the foliage. Three stems of Amaranthus occupy a central position cascading through the design, the lowest pieces coming forwards over the Hosta leaves. Begin to add the longest trailing flowers, in this case Roses, to the extremities of the shape. It is important to step back several feet to view the effect. When you are close, busily arranging, your line of sight is very different from the one from which an arrangement of this size will be viewed.

Step Three

Canterbury Bells come next, slightly shorter and some placed centrally coming forward. Once again make sure the shape is not too convex at the front. Now fill in the central area using large flowers such as Peonies, some cut quite short ensuring good recession to give depth to the arrangement. Step back a few paces and check again.

Step Four

Finally include all the remaining Roses. Check their disposition. It is no good trying to persuade a left-handed sweeping Rose to go on the right. As you fill in a space with a flower, another space will present itself, but make sure there is good balance by equally distributing the quantity. It is worth noting that two small flowers will often balance one larger one, if the large flower is placed lower down in the design as it appears to be visually heavier. Stand to the sides and double check there is enough material of interest at the sides and back. The arrangement must not look like the remains of something sawn in half. Check for gaps and any exposed mechanics and tidy the back. Walk away and look again at the outline and the balance before you finally pat yourself on the back.

BASIC
TECHNIQUES

~

THERE ARE FLOWERS FOR SALE everywhere nowadays and we are bombarded with impulse buys at every turn. I do not wish to knock any of the outlets which encourage the habit, but there are a few vital things to watch out for. Generally speaking, cut flowers do not enjoy strong draughts, cold and severe changes of temperature, or exposure to strong sunlight. All these factors can be troublesome when making a purchase from an outdoor vendor. By all means be attracted by the flowers on the doorstep of a shop, but select yours from inside.

It also pays to check whether the pollen is ripe when the anthers are visible; a bloom is very near its life end when it begins to shed the pollen. So choose stems with slightly closed flowers of clear bright colour, good strong turgid foliage and supportive stems. Avoid buying from a bucket that is very tightly packed: air should be able to circulate round stems to eliminate any mould. Don't let these hazards put you off, however, the joy of a fresh bunch of flowers will lift the heaviest heart and the act of arranging them, however simply, can be very therapeutic.

When you begin, it is difficult to assess the length to cut the stems, so cut them in stages. It is difficult to put a bit back if you have been too drastic. Don't be tempted to cut all the side stems for a posy at the same time to the same length. It may look like a safe bet but some stems may curve more than others and drop further down appearing shorter. You learn with each cut. Deciding how many flowers you need for a certain arrangement is another difficult thing and one not easy to teach. It comes back to assessment. Try closing your eyes, imagining what you want to achieve and counting out what you see.

You begin with a bunch of flowers, a pair of scissors, a vase and some water.
You will develop your favourite pieces of equipment which will make you feel
more comfortable with the task in hand. This is justification in itself to treat
yourself to a Victorian watering can or an ancient trug.

BASIC TOOLS AND EQUIPMENT

All you really need to begin flower arranging is a pair of floristry scissors and a vase, but there are a few other tools which make life easier and, once acquired, you cannot do without. It is worth getting a tool box together and eventually you will probably need two: one for the basic and one for the more advanced tools. Here is a selection of basic tools you will find invaluable:

Anchor tape – this is used to hold wet foam in a container and sticks best to itself. It comes in two widths and in either green or white.

Buckets – tall and short varieties are available and all should be kept very clean. Bacteria from decaying vegetation can drastically shorten the vase life of a flower.

Candle and matches – stems which ooze white latex, such as *Euphorbia*, need to be singed before being put in water, so it is a good idea to have a candle stub and matches to hand in your tool box.

Containers – cheap plastic saucers and bowls are some of the simplest containers for beginners. Candlecups are designed for use with candles and make a footed container.

Dry floral foam – this is used with dried flowers and is available in many shapes including bricks, cylinders, spheres, rings and cones. Choose a make that is less dusty if possible.

Floral fix – extremely sticky material used with plastic foam holders. Once stuck, it is very difficult to remove and can leave a mess, but it is useful if the container is not valuable and is helpful for securing candles.

Floristry scissors – either snub-nosed or pointed, sharp scissors will cut wire netting and wires, as well as tough woody material. If you are serious about floristry, kitchen scissors just won't do. Cutting with inadequate scissors leaves ragged edges to the cuts and this limits the flow of water and nutrients to the head of the stem.

Foam holder – long sharp pins on a heavy base, used to hold a piece of foam in place. They are very secure, but when used with heavy materials, use anchor tape as well.

Hammer – a small hammer is very useful; the one in the picture is almost a family heirloom. You will find a million and one uses for it.

Knives – European designers use knives frequently and I find them light and versatile too. When you buy a knife be sure the blade has a lockable collar or cannot be accidentally shut up with your thumb or finger in place. An old carving knife is also useful for cutting foam blocks to size.

Paint brush – a soft brush can be used for smartening up old containers, and also for brushing away pollen or compost.

Pin holder – for modern designs with strong vertical lines, these are excellent. Flowers stems are stuck straight onto the pins. A good one will last many years; the one in the picture is forty years old.

Reel wire – both black and silver wire are useful for tying in wire netting. Reel wire comes in a number of different gauges.

Secateurs – when brute force won't work on woody stems, conserve your floristry scissors and try secateurs.

Stem tape – slightly sticky, green crêpe paper for covering wires.

Sticks – kebab and cocktail sticks are useful for supporting fruit and

mounting hollow stems. Split bamboo is unaffected by moisture and is the best choice. Together with anchor tape, they are an effective mount for candles.

Stone – remember that it is easier to cut yourself with a blunt knife than a sharp one, so a honing stone helps avoid accidents.

Straight scissors – for cutting ribbons and fabric. Floristry scissors have a saw edge and cannot be used on fabric once they have been used on flowers and wires a few times.

Stub wires – these are pre-cut lengths of wire used for mounting fresh and dried material. Use 18 gauge for stems, 20 for less heavy support and 22 for making bows.

Tape measure – useful for checking proportion and invaluable for competitions.

Watering can – a large and a small can will both be useful.

Wet floral foam – this is designed for fresh flowers as it can hold water above the water line. Only use a block two or three times as it harbours bacteria which shorten the life of flowers. Do not allow it to dry out completely as it will not resoak as well. Store in a sealed polythene bag between uses.

Wire netting – 2 inch (5cm) mesh is the best, but it is difficult to buy in small quantities. Don't be tempted with a smaller mesh, as once crumpled, you will have more wire than holes.

1. Wire netting 2. Wet floral foam 3. Knife 4. Floral fix 5. Dry floral foam 6. Stub wires 7. Secateurs 8. Reel wire 9. Pin holder 10. Foam holder 11. Knife 12. Floristry scissors 13. Hammer 14. Straight scissors 15. Tape measure 16. Plastic saucers 17. Stem tape 18. Anchor tape 19. Knife 20. Stone 21. Candle and matches 22. Candlecup 23. Old paint brush 24. Sticks

ADVANCED EQUIPMENT

As your skills progress, you will find the need for other tools, some of which will just be refinements of ones you already have, while others will extend the variety of the work you can do. You will learn to adapt equipment from other hobbies, so just because something is not featured here, it does not mean you will not find a use for it. Many committed flower arrangers find themselves building extensions or even moving house just to accommodate their equipment.

Bradawl – a great help for making holes in dried materials, bark and driftwood, and even tough fruit and vegetables, ready for mounting on sticks.

Brush – a soft, long bristle brush is a great boon when doing competitive work for eliminating all the little bits of material littering up the allotted space.

Craft knife – as you begin to make accessories for your arrangements, craft tools become very important.

Cut flower food – an additive worth using to get the very best from your flowers. Some flowers, such as Lilac and Mimosa, are actually sold with a sachet attached and certain large stores include one with all their flowers. Flower food can also be bought in bulk packs.

Door wedge – invaluable when unloading the car if arranging flowers anywhere other than your own home. Remember not to leave fire doors wedged open.

Foam holder – larger and heavier than the one in the basic tools section, it is for larger pieces of foam. It could also be used as a counter balance when heavy material is placed in the front of the arrangement, causing instability.

Glue gun – once you have used a glue gun, you can never manage without one. It means instant fixing of stems on dried material, broken vases and damaged driftwood. Solid glue sticks are pushed through a heated reservoir, and melted glue comes through the nozzle of the gun. I prefer glue guns without a trigger action as I find them lighter and more controllable, but this is very much down to personal choice. Remember that the nozzle and melted glue can give a severe burn.

Glue sticks – depending on the type of glue gun you have, either with a trigger or without, glue sticks are either long or short.

Gutta-percha – an advanced form of stem covering, this is a smooth, very elastic tape with a more water-resistant nature. It is used for wedding bouquets and corsages as well as finishing off wire mounts for dried flowers.

Hacksaw – when graduating to huge displays, some stems become too much for humble secateurs.

Nylon line – when an invisible support is needed for drapes or accessories, this is a great help. Fishing tackle shops are a good source.

Old gloves – the prettiest branches are always those with the longest thorns. An old, tight-fitting leather glove will enable you to use scissors or a knife to dethorn a stem without getting in the way. The glove in the picture was inherited from my mother.

Pliers – just a very versatile piece of equipment.

Screwdriver – once you start using electrical tools such as a glue gun, you

will need the wherewithal and tools to deal with a plug.

Staple gun – to be able to prepare bases and backgrounds for arrangements, this is an essential piece of equipment.

Staples – it is worth remembering to check that you have enough staples of the correct size. Boxes tend to be flimsy so tape around them to prevent them falling apart; there is nothing worse than trying to reload a staple gun with tiny lengths of staples that have dropped out of the box.

Tubes – plastic extension cones are useful for making very tall arrangements as they effectively increase the length of a stem. These are usually mounted onto canes with anchor tape.

Wire cutters – as your arranging becomes more ambitious, you will begin to use heavier gauge wire, and your scissors will only take so much strain.

Wreath pins – these strong, sharp hairpins of wire secure moss to wreath bases and floral foam, and the compost on top of planted arrangements; a real aid to disguise.

1. Hacksaw 2. Door wedge
3. Glue gun 4. Gutta-percha
5. Nylon line 6. Glue sticks
7. Wreath pins 8. Bradawl
9. Cut flower food 10. Pliers
11. Staple gun 12. Staples
13. Craft knife 14. Wirecutters
15. Screwdriver 16. Brush
17. Foam holder 18. Old glove
19. Tube

CONTAINERS AND MECHANICS

A container for flowers can be almost anything that can be made to hold water from an old boot, a bucket, a bowler hat or a basket as well as the more mundane bowl. Now we have polythene, anything is possible and with the advent of foam, more of which later, an innovative arranger can work miracles. The only problem is that once you start flower arranging, no cupboard or shelf is ever empty again as you begin to collect. Junk stalls, jumble sales and thrift shops take on a whole new meaning, beaches and riverbeds reveal wondrous pieces of wood, and even bonfire heaps are known to yield amazing charred roots or twisted branches. When I say leave no stone unturned, I really mean take the stone as well as it is bound to come in useful somewhere.

Whatever you use, whether it be conventional or obscure, it needs to be clean inside and that means bacteria-free. The current mania for rusty containers obviously precludes cleaning the outside of a metal urn, but the inside can be scoured or at least lined with clean polythene. There are proprietary products for cleaning vases and buckets, but washing up liquid and a touch of bleach will do the trick as well. Make sure, though, whatever you use, the container is rinsed out well.

Now to mechanics. Firstly wire netting. The best is 2 inch (5cm) mesh netting approximately 12 inches (30cm) wide as this is the easiest shape to handle. Some people like to cut off the selvage edge as the gauge of the edging wire is always heavier, but I have never really appreciated any advantage in this. For me it just makes extra sharp ends on which to impale unsuspecting fingers as you manipulate it. Whatever the mechanics, it is really imperative that they are securely fixed into the container before you begin to arrange. In the case of wire, it is best to tie it in with reel wire unless it is being used in a glass container, in which case anchor tape is more easily hidden.

Pin holders are mainly used for more linear, modern designs and in Japanese style arrangements. I have to admit here that they are my least favourite form of mechanics and that is why I have failed to use any in this book. I prefer my flowers in a more natural state, generally speaking, and I find wire and foam actually give me a better result.

Floral foam comes in bricks and small cylinders in the main, but there are specialist shapes too. There are rings in many sizes on bases such as polystyrene or plastic channelling and spheres in many sizes for topiary work. There are sheets of foam, cones and other specialist shapes. You can also buy jumbo blocks which are as big as six standard blocks put together.

Below: Baskets of all shapes and sizes are invaluable as containers for flowers, if you use a liner, but they are bulky to stow away awaiting use. So make the most of them and make a feature such as this in your home. They are then there to inspire you all the time. But take care as collecting baskets can become addictive and they will soon start to take over your home.

Foam comes in differing varieties: wet foam is green in colour and can be bought in a utility grade as well as one for heavy stems (a denser foam). Some companies are now also introducing a foam which soaks in an amazingly short time. Foam for dried flowers is usually brown and varies in consistency from a rather crisp open type to a finer mousse, not unlike the wet foam to look at. The latter type is best for very fine stems which break easily.

Wet foam is often abused as the blocks are removed from their box, on which there are instructional diagrams, in the shop so the purchaser never sees them. Not only have myths grown up around this product but the expectations of it are often misguided as it is not prepared properly. Run a bowl of water and drop the block onto the water and allow it to sink unaided until it is completely soaked and the top surface is level with the water. Take care not to douse the outer surfaces with water before it is soaked as this traps air inside and flowers inserted into an air pocket will die. Never allow soaked foam to dry out as it then loses the one property for which it is unique – the ability to hold water above the water line. Always leave space within a container for topping up with water. Water evaporates from the foam as well as being used by the plant material, so the foam must be watered regularly to keep the flowers arranged in it fresh.

The technique of using foam is also important. All stems should be cut at as acute an angle as possible to open up a greater space for water to flow through and give each stem more grip in the foam. The stems must be inserted well into the foam, depending on the size of the piece of foam and the arrangement, at least 1 or 2 inches (2-5cm), or more if possible. The outer layer of foam will always be drier than the internal section, so it is logical to try to get the stems in far enough to reach the wettest part. The further in, the firmer the stem is anchored too.

Don't be mean with the amount of foam you use; it is really a false economy. A piece of foam could be used again by turning it over, but after that it tends to be clogged up with nasty bacteria which are detrimental to the vase life of the next batch of flowers, so don't be tempted to reuse foam too much.

The most vulnerable part of a piece of foam is the right-angled edges, so it is a good idea to chamfer the edges to eliminate the risk of them crumbling. This also gives the arranger a bit of extra surface to work in. Treat foam well and it is an invaluable form of mechanic.

Marbles, glass nuggets, gel, sand and moss are all also used as mechanics to hold flowers but are used so little that it doesn't warrant going into further details. Suffice to say that none is difficult to work with should you wish to experiment.

Above: If put away in a cupboard, it is easy to overlook a vase worthy of greater use. So display them on a shelf and enjoy in the meantime.

Above: To mount a candle in a piece of floral foam, use anchor tape to attach short lengths of wooden skewer to the base of the candle to form a series of legs. This enables the candle to stand firmly in the foam without occupying space and inhibiting flower stems to radiate evenly from the centre.

Above: Floral foam comes in all shapes and sizes, some of them quite specific and there are also plastic foam holders on the market. These examples are all made for arrangements to fit on pews in churches. Any could be used for the pew arrangement on page 56.

COVERING CONTAINERS

Cheap plastic containers can easily be converted into rustic wonders or the most sophisticated of vases. All it takes is a little ingenuity and the help of adhesive or reel wire. The two shown here illustrate just what I mean.

Cache pot container

This leaf-covered design looks wonderful as a plantpot holder as well as making a stylish container for flowers. A simple plastic pot is transformed using fresh *Magnolia* leaves which are glued in place with a hot melt glue gun.

Step One
Begin at the top and work round the container in rings, sticking the leaves individually as you go. Trim the little stalks off so the leaves lie flat.

Step Two
For the bottom row, the leaves may need extra trimming so they don't overlap when they are bent underneath. Make sure the leaves are stuck securely in place so the container stands upright.

Step Three
Cut a small circle from a leaf to cover the remaining space underneath. The leaves will slowly dry, so take care later not to damage them. Preserved leaves can be used instead of fresh ones and these will be more tolerant of rough handling.

Mossed pot

A basic container is covered in carpet moss, making a natural, neutral base suitable for many styles of arrangement. This simple technique doesn't even require glue.

Step One
Lay the sheets of moss on the pot and bind on with fine gold reel wire until the sides are completely covered. Don't worry about the base. Carry on binding randomly with the wire to make a gold cobweb effect over the surface of the moss.

RIBBONS AND BOWS

When using ribbon with flowers, either fresh or dried, choose carefully the colour and material and thus the texture. The more expensive the ribbon, the better the finished design. Apart from those types which can be bought ready tied, a good ribbon adds sophistication when used sympathetically. Hessian and linen enhance dried materials well, while rich brocades and velvets lift festive decorations into the extra special.

Tying a perfect bow

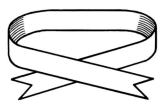

Step One
Make a collar from the ribbon with the two ends crossed at the front.

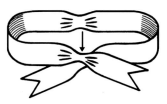

Step Two
Pinch the two ends together where the tails cross at the front, and likewise at the back, then draw the two sides together.

Step Three
Slip a hairpin of stub wire between the tails at the front and pass either side of the bow. Hold in place with your thumb.

Step Four
Draw together the hairpin tails at the back of the bow and twist tightly together two or three times only.

Left: The way in which you cut the end of a piece of ribbon can make such a difference to the finish of a design. A straight cut makes a very hard shape, so try an oblique one instead. This is simple but more effective, but see how much more sophisticated it looks if you exaggerate the angle or turn it into a fish tail or even a swallow tail. Match your ribbon trimming to the mood and style of your arrangement.

CONDITIONING FRESH MATERIAL

Wilting flowers are an arranger's nightmare because they always start to droop when visitors are arriving. The secret to success with flowers is to make sure that all the fresh materials you use are well conditioned before you begin. Ideally, if you pick from your own garden, you should walk round the garden with a bucket of water in the early morning or late in the evening, so the cut material has no time to dry out at all.

Regardless of where you get your fresh material, the golden rule is always to re-cut stems either with a knife at an acute angle, or with scissors at as angled a cut as is feasible, and then cut vertically up the stem and put straight into fresh water in a clean container.

Often it is sensible to put the stems into warm or even hot water. I like to compare my plant material to a child. No-one would put a new born baby in a hot bath, they would use warm water for such a delicate skin. But when the same child has grown a bit and is a rugby-playing teenager, no bath is hot enough! He may come out with a distinct colour change to his rear but he will be invigorated and healthy. In the same way, a new shoot or an emergent leaf will cook like cabbage if put into boiling water but a woody stem will tolerate the experience with just a change in bark colour and will stand up well once arranged. So put new growth into warm water and mature, but wilting, material into very hot water to stimulate each cut stem to drink and, this way, the water to reach the very tip of the stem.

Reviving a 'necked' Rose

Step 1
Fill a small, straight-sided container with hot water. Make sure the water is shallow enough to avoid spoiling the bloom with steam. Re-cut the Rose stem with a knife or scissors and reduce the amount of foliage on the stem.

No flowers like to go from one extreme of temperature to another, so it is always good to experiment with various conditioning methods until you find one which works for you and your plant material.

Remember that, if you are picking from a garden, patience is rewarded. If you desist from picking something until it has matured a bit, it will last longer than if it is picked too young. Back to the child comparison – don't take it away from its mother too soon.

Flowers purchased from a shop or stall should always be stood in fresh water before being arranged as there is no way to tell just what treatment they have had before they were put out for sale. Always choose those which have a clear colour, a turgid feel to the foliage and flower, and with the pollen unshed. Beware of flowers on display out of doors in windy, cold or hot conditions.

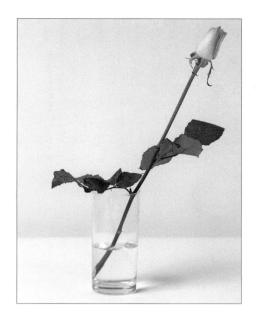

Step 2

Place the stem of the Rose into the hot water and leave it standing. Check it regularly; it should take about half an hour to pick up.

Step 3

The miracle! A strong turgid flower stem just half an hour after treatment. As soon as the Rose has picked up, it can be put into deeper, cold water for a good drink before being used in an arrangement.

SPECIAL CASES

Certain flowers like special conditions. Those which have hairy stems, such as *Gerbera*, prefer only shallow water as do some glaucous foliage flowers like Sweet Peas and Pinks. *Gerbera* also react well to a minuscule amount of bleach in the water to eliminate all the bacteria which block the cells and thus restrict the passage of water. Violets and *Hydrangea* can be floated in water for a while to revive them as they drink through their petals or bracts respectively. Most flowers can tolerate the dark for a while without any detrimental effect, but Chrysanthemums hate the dark and are far better left in a cool, light place.

Proprietary brands of cut flower food do have a beneficial effect on flowers and are worth using. Hellebores, which are always difficult subjects, react very well to conditioning with cut flower food as do Lilac, Guelder Rose (*Viburnum*), Mimosa, and *Bouvardia*.

Flowers which come from bulbs will last quite a time in the cool out of water. Daffodils and Gladioli come straight from the field into the markets and contain enough water to hold. Lilies will do the same, but I feel that once they are re-cut and put into water they develop very quickly. The removal of the anthers from Lilies as they open not only reduces the risk of pollen marking clothes or furnishings but also adds a half day or so on to the shelf life of the flowers. Each flower which has its anthers removed triggers the opening of the next, and so on, so it is often possible to get the whole of the flower spike out before the first flower has died, a wonderful help when a bold form is needed for the centre of a really large arrangement.

WIRING TECHNIQUES

The addition of wire can add extra support when making swags or similar arrangements using either fresh or dried material. The techniques here are also useful for general work with dried and preserved flowers. Wiring of fresh flowers is not normally necessary for general arranging but if you have a bent or slightly damaged stem, or if you need a longer stem, supporting wires can often save the day.

To add a wire stem

Step One

Cut the flower stem very short. Insert a stub wire of sufficient strength (20 or 22 gauge) into the stem and up into the head of the flower. Pass a Rose wire (about 30 gauge) through the flower close to the base. This will hold the petals in place so the flower doesn't blow.

Step Two

Pull the Rose wire down into a hairpin shape and, holding one leg of the hairpin and the stub wire together, tightly wrap the other hairpin leg around the two.

Step Three

To cover the wire, roll the neck of the flower over the end of a piece of gutta-percha, drawing the tape taut and down with your other hand supporting the wire with the fingers. Keep rolling and let the first hand move down the wire in stages following the supporting hand. Roll tightly at the end of the wire and break off the tape. Gutta is self adhesive, but make sure it is kept in an airtight tin to ensure it remains so.

To support a leaf

Step One
With the leaf face down, pass a Rose wire through it half to two thirds of the way up. Draw the wire through until the two sides are almost equal in length, but not quite.

Step Two
Then pull down the ends of the wire into a hair pin, lying parallel with the leaf. Take care not to tear the leaf while you are doing this.

Step Three
Holding the leaf and hairpin firmly between thumb and forefinger, take the slightly longer wire at its tip with the other hand and wind it briskly around the leaf stalk and the other leg of the hairpin, keeping it taut. This is a double leg mount.

Step Four
For a single leg mount, only push the wire through the leaf sufficiently to give one short leg, the same length as the leaf stalk, and one long leg. Proceed as before. You may wish to use two wires together for a single leg mount to maintain strength.

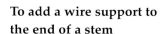

To add a wire support to the end of a stem

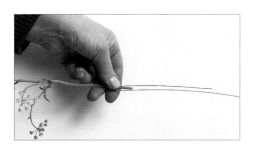

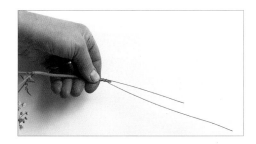

Step One
This effectively lengthens a stem and can be used with fresh or dried material. Hold the stem of the flower between thumb and forefinger about ¹/₂ inch (1cm) from the end. Hold a stub wire at right angles to the stem, then bend down the ends of the wire into a hairpin lying parallel with the stem.

Step Two
Gripping the head of the hairpin and the stem, pull one of the legs of the hairpin out at right angles to the stem and, using a rotary action and keeping the wire taut, briskly wind the wire round the stem and other leg. Pull the leg down parallel again and you have a double leg mount.

PRESERVING

Air drying

Many flowers dry very easily just being 'hung out to dry'. Summer annuals such as Larkspur, and of course *Helipterum* and *Helichrysum*, are traditional candidates. It is worth experimenting with all kinds of flowers; little pompom Dahlias, for instance, dry beautifully. All you need is somewhere dry and airy. An airing cupboard is not the ideal place but often the only really dry place available. Leave the door open slightly to encourage a through draft. A passage of air is vital to successful air drying. An airing cupboard will be too hot and the flowers will dry to a crisp too soon unless you remember to leave the door ajar. The one good thing is that it will be dark which preserves the colour well. A coolish, dry, well ventilated place is the ideal, but make the best of what you have.

A light dusting of borax powder will encourage the colour intensity. *Achillea* reacts well with this method and a yellow which often becomes dull and brownish stays bright and rich. Wherever you hang your flowers to dry, small bunches are best, and pick or choose flowers which are on the verge of maturity rather than fully out. This is the best way of ensuring the flowers do not shed. Lavender is a classic example of a flower which, if harvested too late, will lose all its flowers.

Roses dry well, but do shrink, and the paler colours take on a slightly faded tone. This can be attractive in certain designs but can reduce the shelf life of a dried design when the colours look tired after only a very short time.

It can be an advantage to wire some flowers such as *Helichrysum* before

drying as it is difficult to insert a wire into the head once the flower is dry. Some foliage, like the leaves of *Magnolia* or *Rhododendron*, picked from the ground, can be wired when still damp and manipulated into curves before being put to dry. They will look like they have just dried where they fell.

Hydrangea can also be dried in the air. They should be stood in a container with a small amount of water and then left to dry, but they must be mature enough to start with. Wait until the tiny flower in the centre of the coloured bracts has gone to seed and then try. Earlier efforts may produce crumpled, papery, shrivelled flowers.

As with all off-shoots of a creative activity there is much to learn about this subject and a great deal follows with just personal experimentation.

Above: A nightmare for the rest of the family: gleanings hung up to dry in the airing cupboard. Grasses, Roses and Peonies among others are suspended from a length of broom handle in front of the boiler in a small apartment.

Preserving with glycerine

Preserved leaves stay pliable for a long time – years if treated well and stored properly when not in use. They usually turn various shades of brown from honey to chocolate although, if subjected to strong sunlight, bleach delightfully to cream and off-white.

Prepare a solution of 1 part glycerine to 2 parts very hot water. Use small containers with about 3 inches (8cm) of solution and just a few stems in each. Cut and condition the stems then, having removed damaged leaves and any which might enter the solution, recut the stems and stand in the jars. Top up as the levels go down. Keep in a cool place out of direct sunlight. Preserving usually takes three to five days, or up to eight weeks depending on the plant. The harder and thicker the leaves, the longer they will take. Inspect the jars regularly.

Suitable material includes Beech, Box, *Camellia*, *Eucalyptus*, *Mahonia*, *Moluccella*, *Rhododendron*, *Choisya*, *Pittosporum*, *Garrya* with catkins, *Hydrangea* flowers and Oak.

Large individual leaves can be treated by being immersed in a dish of the solution which, for this method, should be stronger, say 1 part each of hot water and glycerine. Once the leaf has changed colour, it is ready so remove and wash to remove the sticky solution. Dry it thoroughly. *Aspidistra* and *Fatsia* leaves behave beautifully using this method.

Drying with desiccants

In the past, sand was often used as a desiccant and then silica gel became fashionable. There are now several proprietary bands of desiccant; they consist of minute ceramic grains which readily absorb moisture from flowers and leaves leaving a perfectly preserved example almost ready for use. Don't be tempted to leave the materials in the desiccant too long,

however: they become far too brittle and break very easily.

It is beneficial to attach a wire before the process as they become brittle and, once dried, need a coating of a matt polyurethane spray varnish to seal the surfaces as they will reabsorb water if exposed to damp.

Use a deep tin or box with an airtight lid. The desiccant will need to be dried periodically in a warm oven or microwave. Take care if you are using silica gel and a microwave as there are metallic elements which are harmful. The new custom prepared brands eliminate many of these problems and are clean and simple to use.

Flowers to be preserved this way should be young – barely mature is perhaps a better description. There are many, many flowers which preserve well by this method – *Alstroemeria*, Scabious, *Ranunculus*, *Anemone*, *Viola*, *Narcissus*, *Freesia*, Lilies and Zinnias, the list is endless. Ivy leaves and trails and silvery foliages are also very successful.

Using a desiccant

Step One
Pour in a 2 inch (5cm) layer of desiccant and nestle the flowers upright into it. Sprinkle on more desiccant using a paint brush to encourage the grains between the petals. A gentle shake of the container helps settle the contents. Then completely cover with a further layer and put on the lid.

Step Two
After a couple of days, check the flowers. Carefully dig out a sample to see if it is crisp and papery. If completely dry, remove the remaining blooms, if not replace and wait another day or so. The method is quick but some larger flowers may take up to five days. Dust off the clinging desiccant carefully, using the paint brush.

Above: The stem on the left has just been put in a glycerine solution, while the stem in the centre has been there for five days and is ready for use. The stem on the right was treated with glycerine a few months earlier and has taken on a deeper, richer tone.

FRESH
DISPLAYS

~

FOR ME A HOUSE is not a home unless there are flowers around. I relish the changing seasons which bring me new varieties to arrange and enjoy each week. At times I await a late arrival with the anticipation of a child awaiting a new bicycle. Flowers will bring cheer and colour, will comfort, convey love and affection, stimulate, decorate... the list is endless. Quite simply it is the cheapest luxury you can buy. Don't just deck the halls with boughs of Holly, fill every vase with blossom and every pot with blooms.

Arrangements of fresh flowers can be as simple or as complicated as you please, and, as long as they do please you, continue to create them. If you are adventurous, experiment with all kinds of design ideas, if not, stick to what makes you happy. No two blooms or branches are exactly the same so there are infinite combinations of shapes, styles and colour schemes to try out and some will be more successful than others. Working, or should I say playing, with flowers can be a wonderfully relaxing way of accessorising your home and, because the flowers are beautiful in their own right, design failures have still got an awful lot going for them. Anyway, the mistakes won't last very long and some ugly ducklings become swans. A prim glass cylinder of Peony buds, for example, very soon erupts into cushions of soft pink or red frilly petals, too weighty for the stems to bear, and collapses into pools of natural confetti surrounding a green oasis. Three designs from one. Could there be any better value than a fresh flower?

Here some flowers were put in a bucket as though they were being conditioned. The bunches were kept together, thus the flowers were arranged in blocks rather than individually. The collection produces a vibrant and stimulating design while waiting for the arranger. I must admit I don't always have much time to do specific designs for myself, and when this happens I just fetch in the bucket and enjoy it, bucket and all, until I can get my hands on the flowers!

FIRE OF AUTUMN

Warm reddish bricks offer a sympathetic background for a metal basket of Autumn foliage, fruit, berries and seasonal flowers arranged to face the front. The mirror maximises the potential of every stem, doubling up with the reflected image. The colours produced by the changing seasons never fail to enthral me. There is something special about red and yellow leaves, and the fruiting branches provide a whole new section of materials to use. Autumn is a very exciting time so make the most of the riches which will fade all too soon. Dahlias seem to come into their own amongst all these wonderful changelings and I much prefer them used like this than with summer flowers earlier in the year.

RECIPE • metal basket with liner • floral foam • Conkers and husks • Sea Buckthorn
Cotoneaster berries • *Amelanchier lamarckii* • 2 sprays of Wild Rose hip • 5 or 6 Virginia Creeper leaves
sprays of Autumn Raspberry • 6 stems of *Dahlia* • 7 stems of mixed Lilies • 3 Roses • 6 or 7 Apples

1 Soak and trim the foam to fit the liner and chamfer the edges. Use anchor tape to secure if necessary. Fill the space between the liner and the basket with Conkers and husks. Arrange the *Amelanchier* and Sea Buckthorn branches to make the outline, setting the basket at an angle so the handle is neither dead centre nor parallel. Pay attention to keeping a gentle fan shape rather than a triangle here.

2 Allow the Virginia Creeper leaves to flow over the basket edge and cluster them towards the centre to make a focal area. The Raspberry is very special so put it towards the front low down. Blackberry would do equally as well here. Add any remaining berried stems, then begin to overlay the foliage shape with the Dahlias.

3 Arrange the Lilies in the centre, leaving an area in the very middle. Add the Roses in between the Lilies. Mount the Apples on two wooden skewers to prevent them from swinging round. Group the Apples in the central area. Strew some Apples and remaining Conkers at base of the display.

COFFEE TABLE DESIGN

An informal posy of garden flowers arranged simply in a terracotta bowl.
This is an ideal design to be placed on a low table as it is equally effective when
viewed from a standing position as when seated. It adds a very personal
finishing touch to a room.

RECIPE • terracotta bowl • wire netting • reel wire • 7 Polyanthus leaves
small springs of green *Euonymus* • a few small-leaved variegated Ivy trails • 10 *Helenium* flowers
10 stems of Catmint (*Nepeta*) • 5 yellow Roses • 5 or 6 *Clematis* seed heads • 3 *Alchemilla mollis* leaves

1 Prepare the container with the wire netting, securing it with reel wire. Add water. Arrange *Euonymus* and Ivy trails radiating from the central point to make a simple dome. Allow the horizontally-placed stems to make an undulating edge. Add the Polyanthus leaves, spilling out over the rim of the container, standing up slightly towards the centre. Twist the leaves to give each a different plane.

2 Remember to keep turning the arrangement as you work to maintain a balance of material and shape. Place short pieces of Catmint amongst the foliage, following the same shape as the foliage. Tuck in the three *Alchemilla* leaves to add both recession and to cover any unsightly wire.

3 Disperse the *Helenium* through the arrangement evenly. They should be of a similar length. Place slightly shorter whorls of *Clematis* seedheads in between.

4 Finally add the Roses at varying lengths, making sure you turn the arrangement as you do it so these most important flowers are featured on all sides.

FEATURING FOLIAGE

A wonderful copper urn I inherited from my mother. I keep it in a fairly unclean, unpolished state as I love the myriad of colours as it tarnishes: oranges and purples and greens. This way, any materials I add can pick up these colours and are not outshone by bright metal. Here I have arranged a lovely mixture of branches of foliage, some seedheads and huge feature leaves into a quiet, but stately, piece for a grand sideboard. The rosettes of *Choisya* in the middle catch the light contrasting beautifully with the *Hosta* leaves. The forward reaching piece of *Mahonia* is a little wayward, but I could not bear to cut it. The curve of the stem and the lift at the tip seem to possess such bounce.

RECIPE • copper urn • wire netting • reel wire • foliage branches of all or any of the following: *Forsythia*, variegated *Weigela*, *Osmanthus*, *Mahonia*, *Virburnum davidii*, Rosemary, *Cupressus*, *Choisya ternata* 'Sundance' and trails of Ivy • 5 Solomon Seal • 3 large and a few small *Hosta* leaves • Sorrel and Dock seedheads

1 Wire the mesh into the urn and fill with water. Place the *Forsythia* vertically first to set the height, approximately twice the height of the container. Strengthen this area with the Dock and more *Forsythia*. Here I added the curved piece of *Mahonia*; strong Ivy trails would do.

2 Finish the outline of the design. I used Rosemary, *Weigela* and *Cupressus*. Some *Weigela* was placed in the centre coming forward too and the three large *Hosta* leaves were placed centrally and to the side at the base of the design. These give weight to the display.

3 *Virburnum* was added next, to the left, to balance the Hostas. The sculptural Solomon's Seal leaves were repeated down the left side to produce great rhythm and movement. Add extra Hostas and small pieces of foliage to the central area.

4 Add the Sorrel heads next. They link well with the colour of the copper and re-enforce the use of this container. Saving the best until last, set the two glowing pieces of *Choisya* in the middle to bring the whole arrangement to life.

FLOWERS TO GIVE AWAY

Flowers convey thanks and gratitude, love and comfort, sympathy and sentiment. They also cross
all the boundaries of gender, race and religion which gives them a unique qualification as a gift item. Tying
them into a ready-to-use arrangement is such a lovely way to present them and is really not as difficult as it
first may seem. Practice as with so many things is the key to success. Slim stems are a great help when
you begin, as there is a limit to what you can hold in your hand. The spiralling of the stems is the
secret to being able to hold a large bunch.

RECIPE • *Viburnum tinus* • 10 *Achillea* 'Moonshine' • 5 Roses • 3 stems of Guelder Rose • 10 red Tulips
5 stems of *Protea* 'Red Sunset' • 5 *Ranunculus* • 5 stems of Dill • string • ribbon for a bow

1 Prepare all the material, cleaning the stems well and stripping off all the leaves from the lower three quarters. This is essential so that there is no extra bulk to grasp in your hand. Lay the flowers in piles according to variety. This makes it easier to get equal distribution through the bunch when you are making a mixed bouquet.

2 Begin with a shrubby piece of foliage which will give good support. Place the stem at the back of your thumb and forefinger. Add more stems in a spiral fashion. Go on adding and at times turn the bunch round in your hand. Do this by slipping your other hand underneath and gripping the bunch tightly. Loosen the grip of your first hand, turn the bunch a quarter turn with the second hand then grasp again with your original hand. Do this regularly in the mid stages to keep the bunch rounded.

3 When you are satisfied the bunch is balanced, slip the string under your thumb and then bind above your hand a few times pulling the string really tight. Tie securely. Cut the stems level and then cut those in the centre slightly shorter, making the ends into a concave shape.

4 The bunch should stand up on its own. Take a square of cellophane and draw the corners up around the flowers and tie with a pre-made bow of ribbon. Fill the cellophane 'container' with a small jug of water to keep the flowers fresh on their journey to the recipient.

CLASSIC URN

Pedestals and vases on small plinths are the perfect accompaniment for a wedding. This urn is quite wide, thus the arrangement is expansive and fulsome. Both block and urn are fibreglass, making them light to carry. The soft green colour complements any colourway and blends well with stone work. White and cream with perhaps, as here, a tiny touch of the featured colour for the wedding is the most successful scheme during the summer months. It will show up, regardless of where you position it.

RECIPE • urn • wire netting • reel wire • 5 branches of stripped Lime • 7 stripped *Philadelphus* • trails of *Clematis*, Ivy and *Vinca* • 9 *Delphinium* • 3 *Elaeagnus* • 3 white *Hydrangea* • 5 branches of Willow-leaved Pear • 5 Peonies 6 Artichoke leaves • 10 *Eremurus* • 5 Solomon's Seal • 5 Lilies • 6 *Hosta* • 3 *Euphorbia wulfenii* • trailing Rose

1 Carefully scrunch the wire and secure it into the urn using reel wire. Fill with water. Using the Lime, first create the shape making the most of the width as well as the height achievable with the branches you have. Re-enforce the back ground with more foliage, this time the *Elaeagnus*. Put in the trailing forms next, the Ivy, *Clematis*, *Vinca* and Rose trails.

2 Now put in the 'style'. Place the Artichoke leaves and the Solomon's Seal, utilising the natural curving habit by radiating the stems from the central point. Fill the centre with the Hostas, bringing some forward over the rim and add the three magnificent heads of *Euphorbia wulfenii* at the back and to the centre area. Stand well back and check the shape and balance.

3 Overlay the foliage outline with *Philadelphus*, allowing them to flow down where they are naturally heavy and continue this process with the *Delphinium* and *Eremurus*. Now fill spaces in the centre with the Peonies on fairly short stems.

4 Add the Lilies in any remaining spaces, leaving stems longer. I allowed one to fall well down in the front as it had a weak stem and wanted to do that. By putting the Lilies in last, you are protecting them from damage. Stand back and check the arrangement again.

PEW END

Provided the aisle is wide enough, nothing is prettier for a wedding than the attachment of flowers on the pew ends. Cow Parsley is successful as a cut flower if picked when it is fully mature and then carefully conditioned, possibly using hot water treatment. It looks magic in a country church on its own or used with simple flowers in uncomplicated designs. Here I have arranged it with Solomon's Seal, with the leaves removed to show off the little green and white bell-like flowers, and small yellow Roses. I have added a filmy voile bow too, but if ribbon is not to your taste it would still look very effective without.

RECIPE • one third of a block of floral foam • small piece of wire netting • small square of polythene
wire pins made from stub wires • reel wire • Cow Parsley • 9 Roses • 5 or 7 stripped stems
of Solomon's Seal • 6 small trails of Ivy

1 Prepare the base by soaking the foam and wrapping it in the piece of wire netting, hooking it together at the back. Cover the back neatly with the polythene, pinning it in place with the stub-wire hairpins. Double or treble a length of reel wire, make a hanger and attach to one end of the block at the back.

2 Using small pieces of Cow Parsley, make an oval outline, slightly smaller than you wish the arrangement to be. Cover the remaining area of foam with more small pieces. Tuck in the Ivy trails around the edges and a few Cow Parsley leaves. Check that the polythene is disguised by the foliage. It is easiest to do this now.

3 Add the Solomon's Seal flowers amongst the Cow Parsley, then begin to add another layer of Cow Parsley, slightly longer than the first layer. This will produce a lovely frothy look to the design.

4 The Roses will need to be on quite short stems. Place them fairly evenly throughout the design, adding a couple of longer ones at the bottom. Put the pre-made bow into the centre. Double check for gaps. Attach to the pew with reel wire, raffia or ribbon.

COW PARSLEY BALL

This is one of the most effective flower designs ever. It is simple, but a bit tedious, to make but well worth it. Because of the light quality of the Cow Parsley, it is necessary to build up the density in layers to the full frothy, lacy sphere. Short cuts result in the final design not containing enough depth. The secret is to begin with a layer of short-stemmed pieces, then repeat with layers of progressively longer stems. You can use a ready-prepared foam ball or a hanging basket filled with foam as I have done. You must make sure that each stem is inserted into the foam really well to ensure a good supply of moisture. Use individually or in clusters for birthdays or weddings.

RECIPE • 10 inch (25cm) hanging basket • quarter of a jumbo block of foam • Cow Parsley

1 Soak the foam and trim to fit the basket. Do not use a liner. Suspend the basket from a strong hook while you work. The Cow Parsley must be well conditioned using hot water to ensure it will stay firm. Make the first layer using short lengths of Cow Parsley all over the block establishing a rounded shape.

2 When the first layer is even without any gaps, continue with the next layer, using slightly longer stems. When it becomes difficult to hold steady, spike the foam with a stick and use this to support the ball while adding more material.

3 Using longer stems of Cow Parsley, make a third layer, checking all over for gaps. Water it well, allow to drain over a large tray and then raise into position. This design will last a day easily, and if it can be watered and left to drip, it will keep quite well for several days.

FRAMED GARLAND

Planning flowers for a party where space is likely to be in short supply
is a problem. Using a hanging garland on a wall or door solves the
problem. Take care that the back of the garland is sufficiently
protected so that no damage is inflicted where it is hung.

RECIPE • length of plywood cut into an arc • 3 or 4 blocks of foam • 1 thick bin liner (optional) • wire netting • reel wire • hairpins of stub wire • 12 or 15 stems of Leather fern • 6 heads of red *Hydrangea* • 6 stems of purple Michaelmas Daisy • 20 deep purple *Anemone* • 20 short yellow Roses • length of rustic rope

1 Soak foam and cut pieces to fit the arc of wood. Place a complete block in the centre, then work up the sides with smaller chunks. Chamfer the edges and cover the whole thing with a length of wire netting, weaving the two edges together at the back of the wood using reel wire. If the finished design is to hang against a precious surface, cover the back with a bin liner. Lay the arc on top of the polythene, draw it up the sides and pin into the foam using wire hairpins. Cut a bit of rope to make a hanging loop for each end and tie on securely.

2 Hang the garland base up if you can, either where it is to hang when it is finished or in a temporary place, as it is easier to work with it hanging than flat on a table. First disguise the foam with pieces of Leather Fern which has been cut into two or three pieces per stem. Tuck the *Hydrangea* into larger spaces, making sure the stems are inserted securely into the foam – at least 1 inch (3cm). Loop the remaining rope and pin into the garland with large wire hairpins.

3 Cut the Michaelmas Daisy into short lengths and add to the foliage base at random. Add the *Anemone* and Roses in the same way. Spray with water all over, and refresh regularly thereafter by balancing a few ice cubes along the top of the foam to be slowly absorbed without spills.

ADVENT RING

This is a variation on a traditional seasonal design. It is a decorative piece without the religious interpretation. I find it very satisfying to use four candles, making a square pattern inside a circle shape. If you imagine all the shapes, colours and sizes of candles available, as well as all the other festive ribbons and bits and pieces, the design potential is almost infinite. An advent ring is a very acceptable pre-Christmas gift. Remember never to leave a lit candle unattended. Even fresh materials will burn and artificial materials are especially vulnerable.

RECIPE • 1 Pine ring (I cheated here and bought a pre-made one) • 4 candles • wooden skewers
anchor tape • 8 cones mounted on wire • 4 bunches of small berries • 4 bunches of large red berries • 4 tiny wicker rings
4 bunches of Acorns • 4 glitter stars mounted on wire • 4 pre-made bows • wire pins

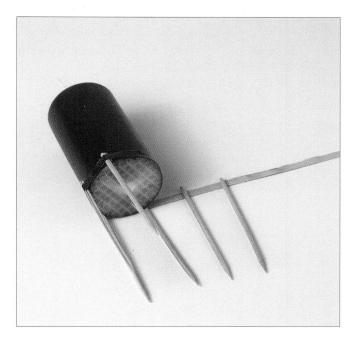

1 Cut off a length of anchor tape and lay it, sticky side up, on the work surface. Shorten wooden skewers, retaining a pointed end on each. Arrange the cut ends of the skewers evenly along the anchor tape and push down to stick.

2 Lay the candle on the end of the tape and wrap the tape around the base of the candle to hold the skewers firmly in place. Repeat with the other three candles.

3 You could make your own Pine ring by binding handfuls of moss to a wreath base using reel wire then, when it is covered, binding on small pieces of Pine, in much the same way as the Pine garland is made on page 67. Fix the candles evenly around the Pine ring.

4 Cluster the decorative pieces around the candles in a repeated pattern. To make it less formal, I twisted the pattern a bit at each candle. Some of the items were already grouped together, some needed to be mounted on wires and the wicker rings were just pinned into place.

CHRISTMAS STAR

Here is a door or wall decoration with a difference. It is easily made and could
be stored and re-used another year. The twigs will shrink slightly, however, so
you may need to bind again with fresh coloured wire. Just add this over the
original wire: you don't need to unwind it.

RECIPE • 3 or 4 handfuls or bunches of Birch twigs • star wreath frame • a stem of Blue
Pine • coloured reel wire • a few fresh or artificial berries such as Holly or
Cotoneaster • stiff hessian bow

1 Attach the reel wire to the inner edge of one of the star's arms.
Take a handful of twigs and trim them to just longer than the star's
arms. Place them over the frame on one of the arms and bind on
tightly with the coloured reel wire. Bind securely right to the tip and
then bind back crossing the other wire and tie off. Repeat with the
next arm of the star using twigs of a slightly different length.

2 Complete all the arms in the same way, varying the length of the
twigs. Curve the points slightly by bending into shape.

3 Cut some short pieces of Pine and tuck into the wire and twig
conglomeration in the middle of the star, radiating out the pieces
as you would with a posy bowl.

4 Tuck in some berries and attach a bow. For instructions on how to
tie a perfect bow, see page 37.

PINE GARLANDING

Making a bound garland on a rope is not difficult if you follow a few golden rules. Firstly make sure the rope is heavy enough for the foliage. Pine is heavy and thus I needed a thick rope here. Secondly, cut the Pine into equal lengths, not too long. Lastly, bind very tightly with the reel wire. This technique can be used with many different materials but is highly suited to evergreens. Don't be tempted to make very long lengths as it becomes difficult to handle. This garland has been attached to a door frame, using the star from the previous page to decorate the door. The star was dressed with fresh pine and a different bow.

RECIPE • Blue Pine • length of rope • reel wire

1 Measure the required length of rope and add sufficient to make a loop both ends. This makes it easier to hang. Cut up the Blue Pine into pieces about 4-6 inches (10-15cm) long. Tie a loop in both ends of the rope.

2 Attach the reel wire to the rope just under a loop and lay a piece of Pine onto the rope and bind. Make sure you bring the wire from under the rope towards you and then pass it over the top away from you and back underneath, giving a sharp tug at the end of the action. This keeps the binding tight and is an important part of the technique. Continue adding pieces, rotating the rope after each to ensure an even garland. Each piece should be an inch (2cm) or so below the last one but, if necessary, add an extra one at the same level if it looks a bit thin.

3 Work to the end of the rope. When you get to the end loop, add some pieces of Pine facing the other way to cover the loop and form a returned end. You may need to shorten some pieces to fill in between, but with careful binding, you should achieve matching ends.

4 Either hang the garland in a loop on its own or with others along a wall, up a banister or lay it over a mantelpiece. Alternatively, frame a doorway with it. Cones or other decorations can be added as you work along the garland if you require a more colourful effect.

CHRISTMAS TREE

There are so many beautiful things which enhance a tree. The lights available have never been better; the more lights on a tree the more spectacular it will be and the fewer decorations you will need. Choose a tree with enough spaces between the branches to suspend decorations and allow them to hang freely. It is easier to start with a good shape, but it is possible to trim a tree to shape and to thin the branches if necessary. Decide on a theme for your decorations and stick to it. It is always tempting to put on all the bits which have been handed down for generations. I always have a second tree for sentimental pieces and then decorate my best tree to co-ordinate with the rest of my decorations.

RECIPE • 1 Blue Pine tree • 4 strings of white pea lights • green twist ties • green stub wires • gold twigs • 10 yards (metres) of gold mesh ribbon • 10 bunches of dried gold Statice • 4 gold papier mâché angels • 10 copper baubles acrylic icicles • 16 gold Apples • 10 gold Walnuts • 6 bunches of gold Grapes • clear glass teardrops • 3 copper bows

1 Pot the tree and trim or thin if necessary. Put the lights on first and use green twist ties to attach them at intervals to the branches. Switch on the first string of lights and attach the first lamp, nearest the plug, to the tree low down and close to its trunk. Take the string out to the end of the branch and wind it gently back to the trunk and then out on the next branch and so on. Start the next string where the last ended; continue until the tree is lit. Thread the gold-sprayed Willow twigs into the tree following the angles of the tree branches.

2 Halve the bunches of Statice and tuck each bundle into the tree, pushing them into the centre to fill the area close to the trunk with gold. With a thin tree, this works wonders filling up empty spaces. Make a bow with some of the gold ribbon and attach to the tree top, then zig-zag the remaining ribbon down and around the tree. Fix the ribbon to a branch occasionally with a green tie. Although this tree was to be viewed from one side only, I dressed it on all sides to give it a more finished appearance and a greater sense of depth.

3 Now add the linear items to the tree on the branch tips and sink the cherubs deep amongst the branches. If you have any extra pieces of foliage removed from the tree earlier to shape it, they can be wired to the top of the tree to thicken it if it looks weak.

4 Hang the remaining decorations in the spaces using one type at a time to get the balance right. Place some on the edges and others really deep into the tree. The copper bows were placed following the line of the trunk. Wrap the base in gold cloth to disguise the pot.

NEW YEAR STOCKPOT

After the extravagancies and rich colours of Christmas, it is refreshing to make a crisp, cool design. Fresh flowers are more often than not very expensive at the beginning of the year, so I often use fresh vegetables and cut houseplants with just a few flowers. This design is well suited to a kitchen eating area, but could be used in a more formal atmosphere, perhaps changing the rope for a silk cord or a velvet ribbon. It is an interesting accent and easily takes on a sophisticated air.

RECIPE • salt glazed pot • large piece of foam • plate or disc for base • 6 trimmed Leeks • 1 short string of Garlic
1 head of Fennel • 2 heads of Broccoli • 1 potted *Syngonium* • 2 small Turnips • 5 small Jerusalem Artichokes • a few
Pecans • 2 pieces of Contorted Hazel • 2 stems of *Euphorbia fulgens* • rough twine • stub wires and wooden skewers

1 Prepare the container, adding a liner if necessary. This one has a small bucket as a liner as there is a hole in the bottom of the pot. Soak the foam, trim the edges and wedge it firmly into the container. The top of the foam should stand above the rim of the pot. If necessary, cover the top of the foam with a small piece of wire netting and secure it to the pot with reel wire.

2 Trim the Leeks to equal lengths. Stand them up around one side of the pot and tie in place with the twine. If you have trouble securing them, use a small piece of double-sided sticky tape on the pot to hold the leeks while the twine is wrapped round and tied. Lay the Garlic string over the top and, if necessary, pin into the foam with wire hairpins. Similarly, pin or wire the two lengths of Contorted Hazel in place. Place the pot on the base before it gets too difficult to handle.

3 Mount the Broccoli and Artichokes on skewers. Arrange the Broccoli to the back, with the heads facing forward, and group the Artichokes towards the front of the display to disguise the pinning or wiring of the Hazel and Garlic.

4 Mount the Fennel and add to the top. Place the *Euphorbia* stems to one side and fill in on the opposite side with leaves cut from the *Syngonium* plant. Loop together some more twine and wind it through the display. Trim the Turnips and add to the base with the Pecans.

71

POT ET FLEURS

This is a design with great versatility. It can be temporary, literally for one night, but is also suitable for a more permanent display. At home, I have various plants around the house and can, in an emergency, gather them together and arrange them in one container with additional flowers for a spot of colour. The simpler the combination, the easier it is to put together. If you want a more permanent arrangement, new flowers can be added as necessary and removed once faded. The plants can be arranged to look good even when the flowers have been removed. Remember to water each plant individually according to its own requirements.

RECIPE • large basket • polythene • moss • small piece of floral foam • stub wires or wreath pins
1 potted *Calathea* • 1 potted *Dieffenbachia* • 1 potted *Pteris* fern • 2 potted *Scindapsus*
2 potted Ivies • 6 stems of Gladioli

1 Line the basket with a sheet of heavy duty polythene – a garden refuse bag is very suitable. Don't rely on polythene already in a lined basket as it is so easy to puncture it. The plants were chosen for their differing forms and the blocks of texture they make. Place the tallest plant at the back – in this case it was the *Calathea*.

2 Place the *Pteris* to one side and the *Dieffenbachia* to the other, packing them in firmly with moss around the pots.

3 Place the *Scindapsus* together in front of the *Pteris* and the Ivies in front of the *Dieffenbachia*. Soak the foam and cover the base with polythene pinned in with wreath pins or hairpins of stub wire. Tuck the foam parcel in the centre, using moss to pack everything together.

4 Arrange the Gladioli in the foam, graduating heights and keeping the stems almost vertical. The group of flowers gives a strong linear movement to the centre of the arrangement and the surrounding plants offer positive areas of texture in both soft and bold forms.

73

A SIMPLE WELCOME

This is a simple design to lift the spirits of any guest who has travelled through the winter weather to make a visit. The Snowdrops are arranged in a Victorian metal eggcup, about the right size to accommodate a goose's egg. The delicacy of the Snowdrops is best appreciated when there is space left around each flower, so you won't need very many for this arrangement.

RECIPE • a good handful of Snowdrops • 6 to 8 small trails of Ivy • 3 to 5 medium-sized
individual Ivy leaves • wire netting • small footed container

1 Cut a small piece of wire netting and scrunch it up lightly. Push it into the container, then wire it in with reel wire to secure it in place if necessary.

2 Arrange the small Ivy trails around and over the edges of the container with three or so at a more vertical angle. Tuck the individual leaves in between to produce a slightly denser centre.

3 Add the Snowdrops between the Ivy trails and leaves, placing some around the outside and others in the centre of the container, varying the angles to add interest. Leave space around each of the Snowdrops to show off the delicacy and the form of each little flower.

VALENTINE'S DAY

This is not the cheapest design to do for a touch of sentiment, but it may just have the desired effect.
It would be a very special arrangement for a wedding or anniversary. Red Roses are the traditional way of
expressing true love, while white ones depict pure love. When used together, they stand for unity, so this design
could even be made with one red and one white heart. The Roses will dry nicely if you allow the
foam to dry out and place the arrangement somewhere warm and airy.

RECIPE • about 80 short Roses – the number will obviously depend on the size of the basket and of the Roses
double heart basket • 2 or 3 blocks of floral foam • soft voile ribbon • glue gun and glue

1 Plug in and switch on the glue gun. Soak the foam and cut it to fit the basket. Chamfer the edges. This is one occasion when the container needs to be filled with foam without any spaces. Watering is easily maintained by drizzling it between the Rose heads.

2 Cut the Rose stems down to about 2 inches (5cm) and methodically insert them around the edges of the hearts, keeping them close to each other and level. Push them right down onto the foam. Then gradually fill in the centre space.

3 Finish filling in the centre area. Try to keep the Roses evenly spaced and as close together as possible. None of the foam should be visible when you have finished.

4 Add a band of ribbon to the basket sides, lightly gluing it in place with the glue gun. Make a small bow, either tied with ribbon or made with a wire as shown on page 37. Glue the bow in position at the join of the hearts

SPRING GARDEN

Daffodils are difficult to arrange naturally but this idea, combining a few new leaves, blossom, moss and a small plant, creates a simple little 'garden' design and is just the thing to bring a breath of spring into the house. If the blossom is picked very tight, the arrangement may well last through two successive lots of Daffodils. The same style can be used at other seasons just as effectively but somehow they never have quite the freshness of these first fragile blooms.

RECIPE • flat shallow basket • dish or polythene liner • floral foam • 10 Daffodils with leaves • 2 small branches of blossom • 1 potted Primrose • 3 or 4 sprigs of *Euonymus* • 5 variegated *Arum* leaves 2 small Ivy trails • a piece of bark • Bun Moss

1 Soak and then cut the foam to wedge firmly into the container leaving a space on either side. It was necessary here to reduce the depth of the pieces of foam too. Group the Daffodils and their leaves as though they were growing in a clump.

2 Remove the Primrose plant from its pot, reduce the amount of compost and place the rootball to one side of the foam in the space left, towards the back. Arrange the *Arum* leaves in the foam the other side and add the Ivy trails to flow out from underneath.

3 Add the blossom for height at the back, inserting with care if the foam is shallow. Repeat with the *Euonymus* in front of the Daffodils. A small stub wire just wound around the bottom of the stem will give it extra grip in the foam if you experience problems.

4 Lay the piece of bark across the foam between the areas of plant material; pin it down with wire if necessary. Arrange the cushions of Bun Moss over the foam and filling the empty spaces, and also disguising part of the basket edge for a more natural look.

ARUM PEDESTAL

Here is a small pedestal design with style. It is formal enough that it could be used for a special occasion such as a wedding or uncomplicated enough to have at home. Here it was set into the side of an enormous fire place.

RECIPE • pedestal and bowl • wire netting • 4 or 5 large branches of *Camellia* foliage • 18 white
Arum flowers and 5 leaves (*Zantedeschia*) • 5 or 6 Ivy trails • reel wire

1 Scrunch the wire netting and attach it securely with the reel wire into the bowl. Fill the bowl with water. Begin to make a loose outline dome shape with the *Camellia* foliage.

2 Fill the dome out further with the *Camellia* and add the Ivy trails taking care to bring some out from the back of the arrangement to help produce depth in the design.

3 Place the Arum leaves radiating from the centre of the bowl tilting the leaf surface a little so that they do not appear too flat. Begin to add the Arum flowers to the top and outline areas first.

4 Add the final Arums, cutting a couple shorter to tuck deeper into the centre. Notice the 'hole' in the centre of the final step – it is not so apparent in the larger picture because it is being viewed from a different angle. It is advisable to arrange in situ where at all possible.

81

CROWN IMPERIALS

These wonderfully statuesque *Fritillaria* – Crown Imperials – are at their best around Easter and make a change from the traditionally used Arum lily. They lend themselves well to a contemporary arrangement. They do smell rather musky though so are best placed out of nose reach.

RECIPE • heavy ceramic tank • wire netting • stub wire • wooden skewers • 3 Crown Imperials
leafless fresh Russian Vine • 1 *Monstera* (Cheese Plant) leaf • 1 bundle of Date stems

1 Crumple the wire into the pot, taking into account the thickness of the stems of the flowers. They are fairly fleshy, too, so take care not to slice them on the wire as you put them into the container.

2 Wind the Vine trails into a ring. If the trails are fresh they will bend without snapping. Place the ring over the container diagonally almost as though it is leaning against it. Place the tallest flower in the container through the circle of vine. This one worked out to be about twice the height of the container.

3 Add the remaining flowers at considerably different heights making use of any curve in the stems. The lowest flower comes slightly forward and is really cut quite short. Wire the Date stems together and mount them on a couple of sticks at right angles.

4 Thread in the *Monstera* leaf to one side and add the Date bundle between the leaf and the flowers, pointing forwards. A simple but effective arrangement making good use of form – circles, rectangles and triangles.

SPRING RING

This design allowed me to use small spring flowers successfully in a ring shape. Instead of trying to force tiny weak stems into a foam ring, I choose a flat galvanised tray and produced a circular shape within it using only the twigs as mechanics. It is a fun way to build up a design and makes you appreciate how difficult it must be to build a bird's nest.

RECIPE • shallow galvanised tray • 6 branches of Pussy Willow • 4 or 5 bunches of Primroses • 4 or 5 bunches of Violets • 20 stems of Lily of the Valley • 2 stems of Guelder Rose • a few small heads of Alexanders or Fennel 5 or 6 Seminole leaves or other thin, strap-shaped leaves.

1 Fill the tray with water. Using the sides of the tray as buffers, curve the Willow branches within the confines of the tray sides interweaving them a little as you progress. Remove any small twiggy branchlets which appear too wild, but leave sufficient to maintain the circular arrangement of twigs outside the container.

2 Tuck the whole bunches of Primroses and Violets in amongst the branches in a regular fashion. Trim the flower heads from the branches of Guelder Rose, leaving a short stem on each. Add these to the arrangement in a similar way.

3 Fill in with small pieces of Alexanders and groups of Lily of the Valley. Slide the Seminole leaves in, emphasising the circular movement of the twigs . These are almost woven in. Take care when you move it into position to avoid spilling the water.

TULIPS AND BLOSSOM

Blossom branches have a wonderful free structure and, arranged in a classic glass cylinder, they express themselves
so well. As the blossom develops and fills out, the whole effect changes so it is like having a new arrangement
every day. Here the addition of amazing Peony-flowered Tulips and a few variegated *Aspidistra* leaves focuses
the eye to the centre. A band of broad, open weave hessian ribbon was attached to the container with
double-sided sticky tape to change the effect of the tall lines of the container a little.

RECIPE • tall glass cylinder • 6 to 8 stems of *Prunus* 'Kansan' or other blossom
10 Peony-flowered Tulips • 5 *Aspidistra* leaves

1 Fill the cylinder with water. Cut the branches to manageable pieces and start to arrange in the container, allowing the curving branches to follow their own inclination. You may need to cut some pieces short to fill the centre of the arrangement if the branches are still immature with only small clusters of flowers at the stem ends.

2 Don't be concerned if each additional stem moves the previously arranged ones. There will come a point at which the stems are interlocked enough to hold fast. Just be patient and don't panic. Continue adding stems until you feel the arrangement is full enough and well balanced.

3 Allowing for the natural movement of the Tulips, arrange them in between the blossom stems. The heads are very heavy and the stems bend under the strain. Take great care with these as they are very brittle and it is so easy to snap off a head or two.

4 Thread in the *Aspidistra* leaves, accentuating the centre by making them radiate from it using their curving lines to lead the eye gently in and out of the design. Blossom branches seem to have a mind of their own, but they look so good I can forgive them their self-will.

SWEET PEAS

The perfume of Sweet Peas as you enter a room is amazingly uplifting and a mass of them together with little else is my favourite way of using them. I remember seeing them as a child on my grandmother's hall table arranged in a Rose bowl. She used to put Asparagus foliage or *Thalictrum* with them. I have substituted the modern equivalent, *Alchemilla mollis*. I don't mean the plant is modern, just the almost fanatical use of it in recent years. The container is a plastic cottage cheese pot. My mother ate her way through many of these for my benefit. I do not care for cottage cheese, but the shape of the pot attracted my attention; she was delighted when the packaging changed.

RECIPE • semi-circular plastic tray • floral foam • anchor tape • about 40 stems of Sweet Peas
in four colours • 10 small or 6 large stems of *Alchemilla*

1 Soak and cut the foam to fit the container, leaving sufficient space around it for watering. Tape it in securely. Sweet Peas do not appreciate deep water, so I find they do quite well in foam. Begin with the lightest colour and arrange a low, but wide and flowing, outline making sure some stems drop down well over the edge.

2 Select the next lightest colour and insert the stems in the same way, re-enforcing the outline and adding a few shorter stems to the central area.

3 Now add the *Alchemilla*, placing some stems with the outline material and some shorter and thus deeper in the centre. I made use of some of the stem leaf bracts to help cover the foam at the bottom of the arrangement.

4 Arrange the remaining two colours of Sweet Pea, filling in the centre of the display, and cutting some very short to recess into the focal area. By arranging one colour at a time, it is easier to balance the colour distribution.

LIDDED BASKET

A lidded basket has a special quality. I love lifting the lid and filling it with garden flowers. This type of arrangement brings the garden into the home, with creamy, scented Honeysuckle and ferns and Hostas framing the central area which is filled with white *Clematis*. With the addition of *Buddleja*, too, this would be a haven for bees. The design is loose and natural, just a lovely relaxed collection.

RECIPE • lidded basket • floral foam • plastic liner • 4 fern fronds • 5 large, branched trails of Honeysuckle
4 *Hosta* leaves • 1 *Bergenia* leaf • 4 white *Clematis* • 4 mauve *Clematis* • 3 stems of *Buddleja*

1 Soak the foam and fit the block into the liner. Secure with tape if necessary. I have used a rigid plastic box as a liner and allowed space around the foam for topping up with water.

2 Evaluate the stems of Honeysuckle and arrange them in a relaxed, asymmetrical shape, radiating the stems from a point slightly to one side of the centre.

3 It is not usual to use an even number of flowers or leaves in a display, but I only had four ferns and four *Hosta*. So I used the ferns in a group together to provide height, and the *Hosta* in a group of three and one with the lone *Bergenia* to frame the feature flowers.

4 Place the white *Clematis* in the central area, keeping the largest for the most central position. I turned one of them a little sideways to change the outline shape. Finally, tuck in the touches of mauve in the form of *Buddleja* and *Clematis* around the focal point.

SHADES OF AUTUMN

I spied this lovely terracotta head one day and couldn't resist buying it; it has such
character. Hung on the well-matched brick wall it just cries out for an interesting
mix of plant materials. The arrangement consists mainly of foliage but a couple
of flowers crept in towards the end. It was created at the beginning of
autumn and so some leaves have begun to take on a hint of colour.

RECIPE • terracotta head • floral foam • polythene for lining • *Viburnum* foliage • Male Fern • *Magnolia* foliage
Hypericum berries • Snowberry (*Symphoricarpos*) • Ivy trails • *Cotoneaster* foliage • *Hosta* leaves • Tree Peony leaves
Amaranthus • *Celosia cristata* • *Galtonia viridis* • *Ornithogalum arabicum* • *Euphorbia robbiae* • bark

1 Line the head with polythene. Soak the foam, cut to fit the opening in the head and chamfer the edges. Using wire pins, secure the bark across the foam in a strong horizontal line.

2 Place Ivy trails out of the lower front and sides, trailing well down. Add the *Cotoneaster* and Snowberry to the sides and the *Magnolia*, *Viburnum* and Male Fern to the top section to make a strong outline. The Tree Peony leaves with the pinky edges and two *Amaranthus* flow well over the rim of the container.

3 Begin to fill in the central area with *Euphorbia robbiae* rosettes and *Hosta* leaves. Fill in between the edges and in the centre with a few *Hypericum* berries. The green *Galtonia* almost hides behind the *Viburnum* at the top of the arrangement.

4 Place three *Ornithogalum* heads diagonally through the centre of the display and recess the two heads of *Celosia* just above the rim of the container.

A POTTED TRUG

Very often after planting out the bedding plants, there is an extra tray of something left. A few such *Pelargonium* plants can be made into an attractive arrangement for patio or kitchen without very much effort. A mixture of plants would also give a pleasant effect, although I must admit to preferring a group of one variety.

RECIPE • large trug • 10 to 12 potted *Pelargonium* plants
about 15 small clay pots

1 Pot the *Pelargonium* plants up into the clay pots or, if they will fit, just slip their plastic pots inside the clay ones. Begin to fill the trug with the planted pots. They will fall at an angle round the edges.

2 To gain extra height for one centrally-placed *Pelargonium*, place its clay pot into another clay pot. Continue adding plants to the trug until the pots are wedged in tight.

3 Add two or three extra empty clay pots near the front of the trug, nestling them between the Pelargoniums. The final result is a real country kitchen style design. Remember to water the plants regularly as the soil will dry out very quickly in a small terracotta pot.

A BASKET OF HERBS

I love to have a herb garden just outside the kitchen door but it is not always feasible. I was without a garden to pick from when I did this design, so I have to thank the head gardener at Lambeth Palace for allowing me to indulge in the amazing herb garden there. The result is a basket with many more herbs than one would normally have, but whether your collection is extensive or not, the idea of sweet smelling, soft textured, quiet colour is the same. It will fit unobtrusively in whichever room you choose in the house.

RECIPE • round basket without a handle • plastic liner bowl • wire netting • reel wire • selection of herbs, one or two stems of each, such as *Angelica*, Chives, Parsley, Marigold, Lemon Balm, Sage, Curry plant, French Lavender, Lavender, Opium Poppy, Rue, Borage, Chervil, Mint, Comfrey, *Artemisia*, Thyme, Rosemary, *Alchemilla*, Fennel and Sorrel.

1 Crumple the wire netting and fix firmly into the liner with the reel wire. In turn, fit the liner into the basket. If it is a loose fit, try packing a little moss into the spaces to hold the liner firmly in place.

2 This was designed as an all-round arrangement but, because of the variation in the materials, it was difficult to get any definition. There was not a lot of textural change or contrasting form. Think of the whole as being an area of soft, slightly fussy texture and pick out anything which has a definite shape to use as a feature flower. Begin as ever with the outline material and, where possible, introduce a larger or smoother leaf to provide what contrast you can.

3 Keep on filling in the outline, remembering to flow some materials well over the basket rim and to radiate everything from the centre. Make sure you keep turning the basket around frequently to attain a balanced design.

4 Finally put in those 'feature flowers'. Here they were the Chives, small *Angelica* heads, and the Lavender. Take great care when handling Rue as it can cause quite a bad allergic reaction. Fennel is another plant which can produce a similar condition.

LINEAR DESIGN

In a modern setting, a strong vertical line arrangement is perhaps more suited and, traditionally, this would have been arranged on a pin holder. Now there is foam it makes life much more simple; I never did get on with pin holders very well. Using materials with strong contrasting characteristics and blocking varieties together makes for a design with good, simple, bold lines.

RECIPE • shallow textured dish • half a block of foam • foam holder (optional) • 5 stems of
Gladiolus • 2 *Philodendron* leaves • *Skimmia* berries • large Ivy leaves • roll of
bark (commercially produced) • wire pins

1 Soak and cut the foam, not forgetting to chamfer the edges. Fit
firmly into the dish. Use a foam holder under the foam if you are
concerned about the flowers being too heavy for the container.
Sometimes, as the flowers develop and the foam dries out,
arrangements can become unbalanced and topple over. Place three
stems of Gladioli vertically at differing heights.

2 Add the two *Philodendron* leaves slightly to one side of the front of
the container. Use them together to make one block of material,
facing forward.

3 Pin the roll of bark across the middle of the foam at the base of the
column of Gladioli, using the wreath pins to hold it in place. Add
the other two stems of Gladioli, one either side of the central column
and both cut shorter than the other stems.

4 Cut the berries onto short stems and create a diagonal line of
colour behind the bark. Fill in behind them with the Ivy leaves. A
simple, very quick arrangement.

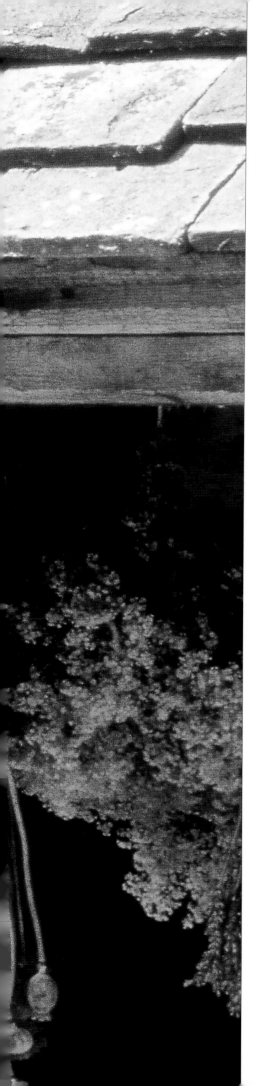

DRIED
DISPLAYS

~

DRIED AND PRESERVED flowers and foliages are invaluable for use in rooms which are not used much or when fresh materials are expensive. Simple bundles of grasses and leaves hung on a wall make a pretty decoration with little effort. Dried materials also make wonderful miniature designs, and huge spathes and fronds make excellent sculptural pieces for large displays.

Working with dried materials can become an obsession. In most homes, the stock of dried materials always seems to end up in a box under the spare bed. Do go through them regularly, though, as one tends to harbour bits and pieces for years and after a time they do begin to deteriorate. It is tempting when taking down a design of dried materials to keep everything for the next display, but they are usually dusty and dilapidated so be firm with yourself. Don't dry too much either because it won't be just the spare bed they are under. It is quite a good idea to make a list or carefully label the boxes as it is difficult to remember just what you have got stowed away.

It is worth remembering that good dried materials are not always a cheap option, particularly if you choose to buy items from overseas, but they are worth collecting and arranging. It is a very different medium from fresh materials. In the main, they will last a year in most cases and in some up to two years, but they do fade and attract the dust and deteriorate. There are proprietory cleaners on the market which do extend the shelf life a bit. If you work on the premise that if you are tired of them, they are probably looking tired themselves so ruthlessly throw them out and you will get the best out of them. Unless, of course, you want to spray them gold for Christmas – dried materials sprayed with metallic paint do lift seasonal foliages at Christmas time and help to eke out the fresh flowers.

Newly-prepared bundles of flowers for air drying, bound with string and ready to hang in a suitably dark, airy place indoors.

FRESH OR DRIED?

This arrangement could be made with dried or fresh material. The only difference would be that the dried materials would have a softer, more muted tone to them than the fresh materials. All the ingredients in this arrangement can be preserved with good results. The Wheat would be air dried, the *Nigella* and Cornflowers would be either air dried or preserved with a desiccant, the Campion seedheads would be preserved in glycerine and the Ivy would be dried with a desiccant. The basket is covered with bark and would be very effective in both dried and fresh versions.

RECIPE • lined oval basket • 10 stems of Wheat • 1 bunch of pink Cornflowers
1 bunch of white *Nigella* • 1 bunch of Campion seedheads
5 Ivy (*Hedera canariensis*) leaves

1 Prepare the foam either in wet state or dry, depending on whether you are using fresh or dried materials. Trim the edges of the foam and place in the basket. Make an oval outline with the Campion and tuck in the Ivy leaves quite deeply.

2 Arrange the Cornflowers and then the *Nigella* throughout the posy, with the stems at a similar length to those of the Campion, but with two or three of the Cornflowers deeper down in the arrangement.

3 Pop in the stems of Wheat which break up the rounded forms with sharp little spikes. Keep the material under the handle so that it is possible to use it. If you are working in dried, you may need a few extra stems of everything. Moss can be used to cover any exposed foam.

FLOWERS FOR THE HEARTH

During the summer months, an empty hearth can look quite depressing and a large
dried arrangement is an ideal way of cheering up the space. In homes with central heating, the fireplace is not
always used, so again this type of design decorates a difficult space in the room. It is best to have
some large flowers in the arrangement to keep scale and proportion correct.

RECIPE • 1 large basket • foam for dried flowers • preserved Beech stems • 6 dried *Celosia cristata* • 1 bunch of dried *Amaranthus* • 6 dried Artichokes • 5 stems of dried Maize • 1 small bunch of Oats • 1 small branch of preserved *Eucalyptus* • 10 dried Roses

1 Pack the basket tightly with dry foam. If you are concerned about the stability of the completed design, put something heavy in the base, such as pebbles or an old lead weight. Arrange a fan shape outline of Beech and *Eucalyptus*. Remember to have some of the stems flowing backwards.

2 Accentuate the outline with the spikes of dried *Amaranthus* bringing some in towards the centre, too. Next group the plumes of *Celosia cristata* centrally.

3 Chose the largest of the Artichokes for the very centre of the display and then arrange them and the remainder through the materials already in the basket. Tuck in the Roses taking care not to snap them as they are very brittle.

4 Add the Maize heads to the design. The gold colour has a lifting effect on the other colours. Lastly insert the Oats into the spaces and this in its turn also lightens the quite sombre colours.

NURSERY RING

This is a simple and subtle wall decoration which would be well suited to a child's bedroom, though of course it would have to be out of reach of little hands. In this arrangement, a tiny teddy bear suffered the indignity of having sheet moss glued all over him.

RECIPE • willow wreath • teddy bear • sheet moss • glue gun and glue sticks • trimmed cones • dried Broomrape • preserved *Clematis* seedheads • Cinnamon sticks • preserved *Eucalyptus* leaves • dried *Helichrysum* • tiny wicker basket

1 Spread hot glue over an area of the teddy. Before the glue dries, press pieces of sheet moss firmly on the glue to cover the teddy, carefully following his contours. Continue with the next area until covered. Take care not to burn your fingers when pressing on the moss.

2 Glue the bear firmly to the willow ring. Next add a few trimmed cones horizontally beneath him and a few sprigs of dried Broomrape behind him. Fill in the areas between the cones and around the teddy with dried *Clematis* seedheads to soften the effect.

3 The design is completed by the addition of short Cinnamon sticks glued into a pile over the cones, and preserved *Eucalyptus* leaves and halved *Helichrysum* heads tucked between the other elements. A tiny basket is glued firmly to the bear's paw.

BOX TOPIARY

Topiaries made from the classic material, Box, are relatively easy
to make and effective additions to most homes. The beginning is a bit messy, so
get out your rubber gloves. It is quite surprising just how much material you need.
This Box topiary took a whole hour's worth of prunings.

RECIPE • **a good quantity of fresh Box foliage** • **1 bent stick** • **1 small bag of plaster** • **1 terracotta pot**
1 dry foam sphere • **Bun Moss**

1 Mix the plaster and fill the terracotta pot to about three quarters full. As the plaster begins to set, insert the stick to form the trunk of the tree. When the plaster is firm, impale and secure the foam sphere on the stick. I used the glue gun to hold it in place.

2 Cut the fresh Box into small pieces and, beginning at the lower edges around the stick, insert them into the foam. They must be very close to each other, really packed well together. When put to dry, the leaves shrivel and if there is not enough density you will be able to see the foam through the foliage.

3 Continue, carefully and methodically, until the sphere is completely covered with foliage. Check again when you think you have finished to make sure there are no gaps or areas which are less dense than they should be.

4 Trim the Box into a perfect sphere. Holes will show up if the stems are not close enough together, but it is still possible to fill them and trim as the rest are trimmed. Cover the plaster with a few pieces of Bun Moss, then leave on display and the design will dry out.

DECORATED FRAME

To make a plain picture frame more interesting, dried and preserved materials can be attached to make the final picture more three-dimensional. I used a small piece of contorted Hazel taken across the face of the frame; it does not inhibit the view of the picture, but adds a little extra depth. All the pieces added were fairly simple so as not to detract from what is in the frame. Frames completely covered in woody seedheads, shells, bark or even moss make striking surrounds, much cheaper than a gilded frame, but often just as effective.

RECIPE • Contorted Hazel twig • 3 skeletonised leaves • a piece of metallic cord • 2 preserved *Eucalyptus* leaves
tiny *Echinops* globes • dried fern • fine blue wood curls • 3 dried Roses • wooden frame • glue gun and glue

1 Roll the skeletonised leaves into cones. Attach two to the corner of the frame with the glue gun. Skirt round the bases of the cones with two individual preserved *Eucalyptus* leaves.

2 Glue the third leaf cone on top of the other two to make the arrangement three-dimensional, then add a few pieces of dried fern behind the cones and running along the frame. Add a few wood curls to soften the effect.

3 Glue the Roses into the leaf cones. Glue in the twig across the frame and tuck in and fix the copper cording in loops. Now add the *Echinops* globes in between. The smaller and more discreet the design, the less it takes away from the contents of the frame.

111

KITCHEN SWAG

A chunky decoration of dried seedheads, preserved fruit, nuts and grass plumes snuggled in amongst rough hessian fabric is just the thing for a kitchen, especially a country one. It conjures up an image of a cosy cottage kitchen, with a low ceiling and warmth radiating from a stove, and cat in the window and a dog on the mat. Chunky dried materials are so much more robust for a busy room than delicate air-dried flowers and they will withstand the rigours of kitchen life.

RECIPE • 1 plank of wood approximately 4 by 24 inches (10x60cm) • dry foam • hessian • dried grass heads •Poppy seedheads • dried Pomegranates • Brazil nuts • dried Orange slices • dried Limes • mini *Lotus* heads • *Achillea* • dried Bun Moss • Bell Cups • *Jacaranda* pods • a small length of string for hanging • glue gun and glue • wire pins • drill

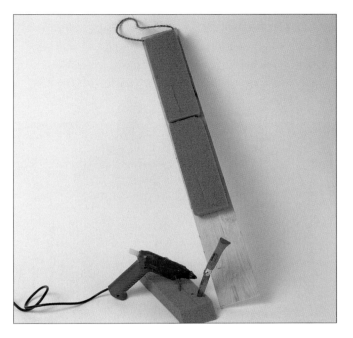

1 Drill a hole at one end of the wood and thread with string for hanging. Divide a block of dry foam into four slices and glue as many as you need to the plank, leaving small spaces between. Depending on the length, you may need more than one block of foam.

2 Pin and glue the hessian in gentle curves down the plank. Following the same curving lines, glue grasses such as Marram or Millet in a river of movement through the length of the drop. Add small groups of Poppy heads at regular intervals.

3 Continue adding groups of materials amongst the fabric. Watch out for the balance and the textural differences between the groups. Fill the sides first with the more neutral tones, leaving the frontal spaces for the exciting materials such as the Pomegranates.

4 Add the fruits and remaining items. Accentuate with clumps of moss and *Achillea*. Leave enough of the hessian swirls showing to give the whole drop some movement. These kinds of designs can be quite heavy-looking, so any strong curves are of great benefit.

WIRED GARLAND

This is an alternative way to make a garland; in this method, all the materials are mounted onto a double leg mount. The flowers are collected into small bunches and wired together; it is preferable that all the preparation is done before you begin to make up the garland. Choose your materials carefully, looking for varied forms and textures and harmonising colours. Most dried garlands made with a selection of flowers will be more fussy than those composed of seedheads. Garlands such as this will give out a very traditional feel. This technique of wiring can also be used with fresh material and should be compared with the technique used on page 67.

RECIPE • stub wires • selection of dried flowers such as *Helichrysum*, Poppy seedheads, small Lavender bundles, Peonies, Rodanthe, Statice and Roses • thin coloured rope to wire the materials and to use as part of the garland

1 Prepare all the dried materials into small, short-stemmed bunches and mount onto supportive wires with a double leg mount. Cluster the Poppy heads in threes; the other bunches should be about the size of a child's fist. Loop the fine rope several times and mount as for the other materials. If you lay out the materials onto a table you should be able to estimate the quantity you will require to make the garland. Cut off a length of rope as long as you wish the garland to be, plus enough to make two loops, one on each end.

2 Start the garland with a wired piece which is full and bushy as it helps disguise the hoop from which you will hang the garland. Lay the piece parallel to the rope. Wind one of the mount legs around the rope and the second leg, binding them together. Turn the rope a quarter turn and add another piece in the same way, just below the first. Turn the rope again and repeat. Check regularly that the pieces are blending and no gaps have appeared; you cannot fill them in later. The Lavender bundles lie across the rope, not along it, but are added in the same way.

3 Continue until you reach the end. Gather several bunches into a small mound and bind together with a mount leg. Bend the stems back at a sharp angle. Add to the end of the garland with the heads in the opposite direction. Bind in and fill the gap with a few more bunches.

SPICE POSY

This is a design idea which has roots in the Tryol. It is a lovely gift to make and is a delight to find on a dressing table as well as around the house. The spicy smell conjures just the right atmosphere at Christmas time too. Patience is required to wire some of the items. Some nuts which are traditionally included are impossible to wire without drilling, but the advent of the glue gun facilitates the attachment of a stick. However, it is possible to buy some of the bits and pieces ready wired. I took advantage of this and used several commercially-prepared items amongst my posy.

RECIPE • posy frill • stub wires • gutta-percha • reel wire • finely coiled gold bouillon • 1 or 2 each of the following: cones, Cinnamon stick, Nutmeg, Almond, dried Orange pieces, Poppy heads, *Lycopodium*, *Achillea*, *Eucalyptus* buds, *Helichrysum*, Beech nuts, small mints, 'spice packs' of Cumin and Poppy seed, artificial berries, Honesty, *Celosia* • gold ribbon

1 First mount all the ingredients not already wired. Add fine gold wire to decorate some and pull out the bouillon and wind round others such as the Beech nuts or the Cinnamon sticks. Gutta the wires if necessary. I prepared about 40 individual stems for this posy.

2 Attach the reel wire to a small stem and begin to bind together the items. Pay attention to the shapes and the textures you put next to each other.

3 Continue to add the pieces to the outside of the posy, turning it round constantly to ensure you keep it circular. Bind in well and finish by binding down the stem with the wire.

4 Make two small bows with gold ribbon. Slip the posy into the frill, then bind in the bows underneath and shorten the stem a little. Cover the stem with gutta-percha or gold ribbon. It may be necessary to secure the frill with a small blob of glue.

LAVENDER POTS

The arrival of fresh Lavender in markets and shops each year is one of the seasonal landmarks. It is available for such a short time. This may account for the amazing popularity of Lavender in its dried state. Traditional Lavender bags and plaited bunches to hang amongst clothes are well known but now modern 'hedges' and terracotta pots stuffed with Lavender are always in demand. Lavender is never cheap to buy, so if you can, grow your own. The flowers need to be slightly immature for air drying or they will drop.

RECIPE • small wooden box • dry foam • 6 or 7 bunches of dried Lavender
raffia • moss • glue gun and glue • a few wreath pins or stub wire hairpins
sharp serrated knife

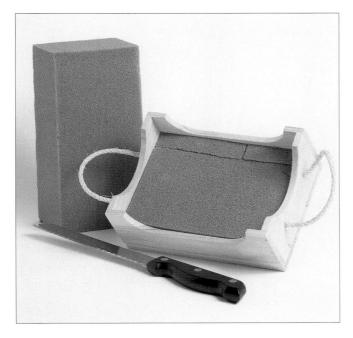

1 Cut the dry foam to fit the box exactly and pack in, keeping the foam level with the top of the box.

2 Select ten, or so, stems of Lavender and cut the stems down to the correct height, including an extra inch (3cm) to insert into the foam. Begin along a long edge of the box and place the small bunch in the foam in one piece. Repeat along the edge and then add another row, and so on, building up a rectangular block of Lavender with parallel stems and all the heads level. Keep a careful eye on the height as it is very easy to end up with a slanting top.

3 When you have filled the box, pack in extra bunches where needed along the sides. There are always a few gaps. Glue a little moss between the box edge and the stems. Take a few strands of raffia and loop them together through a wreath pin.

4 Pin the raffia in loose loops around the join between the box and the stems, allowing some loops to fall a little lower for greater movement. Choose three or four long strands of raffia and tie in a band round the Lavender block about halfway up, knot and trim the ends.

TABLE
DECORATIONS

~

THERE IS NOTHING NICER than a well dressed table. Flowers in the centre turn plain food into a feast and the best into a banquet! When deciding just what to use, take stock of the kind of table – plain or polished wood or glass, with a cloth or just mats, modern or antique, – look at the surroundings, the style of decoration and the colourings. Sometimes it is also worth considering the food to be eaten. Personally I love to use lemons with flowers for a meal featuring fish. Perhaps the food is Eastern, hot curry or a highly spiced dish; bright reds and oranges with dull golds and burgundy echo the concepts we have of Indian food. In summer, when the weather is hot, cool white and green refresh the guests. Table flowers can be casual, formal, simple, subtle, sophisticated – but it is important that they fit in with their surroundings and the meal to be eaten. When they don't, their incongruity can easily affect the diner.

It is also worth remembering that the shape of the table determines what is the best style of arrangement. One round posy in the middle of a long refectory table would look very out of place; two or three would be better. However, one long slim decoration would be an even better choice. If the table is very wide, it is difficult to talk across the table so as long as the design is not too dense, it can be a little higher than one for a small narrow table where you will want to speak to the person opposite you. For very formal occasions, it is both fashionable and very effective to make a design which is raised on a slim stand so you can look and speak underneath. Sometimes, too, it is very pretty to make individual arrangements for each guest to leave the table centre free.

Warm late summer colours enhance the polished wood. Honeysuckle foliage trails make a relaxed outline for a long arrangement, a classic shape for a rectangular table. Golden garden Roses mingle with red and cream Lilies and matching gleanings from an herbaceous border.

SIMPLE SOPHISTICATION

Rough textured, rustic materials team up with pure white Roses and strong leaf shapes around a candle – a real rough with the smooth combination. The shape is deliberately irregular and the grouping is such that no two sides are the same. The colours are cool and relaxing and the design would look equally effective placed on polished wood or a spotless white table cloth.

RECIPE • shallow dish • floral foam • foam holder • candle • wooden sticks and tape • 2 pieces of rough bark • Bun Moss • green and white *Hosta* leaves • small Ivy trails • Spider Plant (*Chlorophytum*) leaves • *Hydrangea paniculata* flowers • *Physostegia* seedheads • white Roses • *Choisya* flowers • *Clematis* seedheads and tendrils • Snowberry

1 Soak the foam, then press onto the foam holder for stability. Chamfer the top edges, then place in the shallow dish. Mount the candle on four pieces of wooden stick using anchor tape. Place the candle centrally in the foam.

2 Push the pieces of bark into the foam, one on either side. Tuck moss into the clefts in the bark. Make an irregular framework of foliage radiating from the centre, using *Hosta* leaves in groups, curving trails of Ivy and *Chlorophytum* leaves. Next add florets of *Hydrangea* recessed into the centre on two sides to accentuate the irregularity, and two groups of *Physostegia* seedheads to add texture.

3 Add the Roses, *Choisya* and *Clematis* heads in groups, continually turning it to keep the design balanced. Finally add a few sprays of Snowberry and finish with a few *Clematis* tendrils running through the arrangement in silky coils of pale green.

FULLNESS OF SUMMER

I was let loose on an herbaceous border for this arrangement, so it contains a myriad of flowers, one, two or three stems of each. This makes it quite difficult to explain a set procedure, so this is a good exercise for putting into practice the principles and elements of design, assessment of the materials you have available, their size in relation to the container and each other. The basket I used is vast. You can tell how large it is when you see that the bowl I used as an inner container is actually my washing up bowl. This is just a glorious collection of summer flowers and foliages; a real tonic if you live in a city.

RECIPE • large basket • washing up bowl • wire netting • moss • a selection of Foxglove, Lily, *Allium*, *Philadelphus*, Beech, *Cotoneaster*, *Hosta*, *Euphorbia*, *Onopordum* leaves, *Berberis*, *Escallonia*, Grasses, Valerian, *Aconitum*, *Delphinium*, *Alchemilla*, *Salvia*, *Iris*, Mignonette, Roses, Cornflowers, *Astilbe*, *Agapanthus*, Russian Vine, *Dicentra*, Peony, Stock

1 Set the basket with the handle at an angle. Crumple the wire netting and place in the bowl. Secure with reel wire or by folding pieces over and under the rim. Hide the bowl with the moss. It probably wouldn't be seen anyway, but it gives peace of mind when using a plastic container. Fill with water.

2 Select pieces of foliage and blossom and arrange a relaxed outline through and under the handle. This arrangement is slightly asymmetrical – one side longer than the other. Bring the bolder shaped leaves into the centre, such as the *Hosta* and *Onopordum*.

3 Sort the flowers into spiky shapes, rounder bolder ones and the rest. Using the first group, incorporate the more linear shaped stems into the outline, not forgetting the front edge. Allow any stems with natural curve and movement to flow over the extremities of the basket.

4 Pick out the feature flowers such as Roses, Peonies and Lilies and group them towards the centre, recessing some under the handle. Fill in between the outline and the focal area with the remaining materials. Place small flowers in groups to give them more impact.

HARVEST SUPPER

A wander around an autumn garden reveals many wonderful things. Take a basket on your arm and scavenge. My foray for this design yielded Sweet Chestnuts, Acorns and dried leaves from the ground, Pumpkins, Mushrooms, Crab Apples and dry twigs... I could go on and on. The revelations of each season are so exciting. Even on a sophisticated polished table, the rustic quality of this design is not lost and does not look out of place. The autumn colours positively glow and the fruits of the season spill out from every side.

RECIPE • plastic tray • floral foam • anchor tape • Pumpkin • Gourds • ferns • *Azalea* twigs with lichen • Horse Chestnut leaves • *Kniphofia* • *Pyracantha* • Chrysanthemum • Terracotta pots • Dried leaves • Sweet Chestnuts • Acorns • Maize • Pears • Crab Apples • fungi • Honeysuckle • small Ivy trails • *Clematis* seedheads

1 Soak foam, trim edges, and tape to the tray. Put the container in situ and strew a few dried leaves, Gourds, Chestnuts and flower pots around the edge. Place one larger pot at an angle on the foam and hold in place by pushing a twig through the hole into the foam. Place the Pumpkin at one end of the block. Arrange the *Azalea* twigs to give both height and side interest. The stems must all radiate from the centre. Add the *Clematis* and Honeysuckle trails flowing from both ends.

2 Surround the large pot with coloured Horse Chestnut leaves. Pile fruits – Pears, Gourds and Maize – in amongst the leaves. Tuck in a few Ivy trails. It is important to walk around the table and arrange both sides in turn. It can so easily become visually unbalanced if you don't. Fill the large flower pot with Sweet Chestnuts and add a few pieces of fern between the pot and the Pumpkin.

3 Next place three or four stems of Chrysanthemum spray around the central part and top the whole design with two *Kniphofia* heads rising between the pot and the Pumpkin like the flames of an autumn bonfire.

4 Now add the finishing touches. Drop in more fungi on the table around the arrangement and strew a few more things, like the Acorns, around. Lastly, tuck in the golden Crab Apples and the stems of *Pyracantha* berries.

SUNFLOWER CIRCLE

Sunflowers have caught the world's imagination recently and here is a design made entirely of
small flowerheads with Goldheart Ivy – a ring of happy faces. It is a low, compact arrangement,
easily made but with maximum panache. It is a perfect design for a conservatory party.

RECIPE • foam ring with base • straight sided glass dish • 25 small Sunflowers
Goldheart Ivy • *Viburnum davidii* leaves • 4 floating candles • glass chippings

1 Lightly soak the ring frame of foam, chamfer the outside edge and slip the bowl into the centre. It just happened that I had one that fitted perfectly, but it is not an impossible task to find a suitable container for this display.

2 Cut the Sunflowers very short and begin pushing them firmly into the foam, filling in between them with small pieces of Ivy and *Viburnum*. Work methodically round the ring rather than haphazardly inserting the material.

3 Continue working round the ring, filling in as you go, altering the angle of the flower heads and remembering to recess the odd one now and again. Once the ring is complete, add the glass chippings to the bowl, fill with clean water and float the candles in it.

LEAF MAGIC

There are times when foliage is enough on its own. In the early part of the year, when the leaves are fresh and the new colours clear and bright, I love trying different collections of leaves on their own. The end result here is by no means green, and I did cheat a bit at the end by adding a few Tulip Tree flowers. I just came across them in my collection of cuttings and the colouring was perfect with the other materials. A foliage table centre is a great help for a busy hostess as it will last well and can be arranged much further in advance than flowers.

RECIPE • shallow lined basket • floral foam • *Mahonia aquifolium* • Golden Privet
Sycamore • *Hosta* leaves • 1 *Anthurium crystallinum* leaf • Ivy • *Artemisia maritima*
Elaeagnus umbellata • 3 Tulip Tree flowers

1 Soak and cut the foam to fit the basket. If it is wedged in well, there will be no need for anchor tape. Radiate small pieces of Golden Privet around the edge of the basket, alternating with a few *Mahonia* leaves. Place a couple of pieces in the centre to establish the height. In this case, the whole design was no more than 8 inches (20cm) high.

2 Add the coloured Sycamore stems to the central area. Sycamore is only this colour when the shoots are young. Position the *Anthurium* leaf and add the *Hosta* leaves in groups around the container rim and into the centre.

3 Fill in any small gaps with pieces of Ivy, filigree *Artemisia* and the *Elaeagnus*. The addition of a touch of silvery grey lifts the other colours. Finally place the Tulip Tree flowers. I had just three for this arrangement. The colour combination is unusual but works very well.

JUST FOR YOU

When a table is laden with dishes of food, an individual flower design for each person is often more effective than a central display. When decorating a very large table with masses of space, additional tiny arrangements matching the main centrepiece add a certain something to the table settings. A tiny design also adds a personal touch to a meal on a tray, and a dressing table for a guest room is far more welcoming with a special little arrangement of small flowers. Fruits, vegetables and leaves can also be used to great effect.

BEAN BUNDLE RECIPE • Green Beans • plastic tube with cap • 1 small Sunflower • green string • LEAF SPHERE
RECIPE • *Ceanothus* leaves • foam sphere • large-headed pins • silver pot • TOPIARY RECIPE • Cornflowers • tiny
Ivy leaves • moss • small pot • floral foam • raffia • DAISY PAIL RECIPE • tiny metal bucket • Marguerites

1 To make the bean bundle, cut the flower stem down to 2 inches
(5cm). Fill the tube with water, fit the cap and push the stem
through the hole in the cap. Arrange the beans around the tube,
aligning the stalk ends. It is best to choose equally-sized beans, but if
they are of variable length, allow the variation at the top not the
bottom. Bind and tie the bundle tightly with the string and gently
adjust or pull out the bean 'legs' so the column of beans will stand up.
Plastic tubes often come with commercially-grown Orchid stems.

2 To make a leaf sphere, start at the top of the sphere, pinning the
leaves to the foam, each with one pin at the base of the leaf. Add
one leaf at a time and spiral the leaves round and slowly down the
sphere until you have covered the ball of foam sufficiently to hide the
foam entirely. There should be no gaps. Randomly add odd pins to
decorate the green ball and place it onto the pot. If you can't get
Ceanothus leaves, any small evergreen leaves will do, especially
Eucalyptus or Ivy.

3 Make the Cornflower Topiary by creating a tiny posy in your hand and tying the
top tightly with raffia. Cut the stems level and insert into the pot which has been
filled with soaked foam. Hide the foam with Ivy and moss. To make the Daisy Pail,
arrange the Marguerites in the bucket, interlocking the stems so they support each other.

FLOWERS FOR A FEAST

For a grand party or special celebration, there is nothing better than a rich fruit and flower combination in sumptuous colours. It may look complicated, but it is quite simple if you follow a few guidelines. Select the fruit in the same way you choose flowers, being aware of scale and proportion, colour, texture and form. If you can, try to make the arrangement in situ. Spread polythene across the table and a towel over the top. A completed design can be hard to lift, especially if, like me, you decide on a heavy metal urn as the container. Designs like these are always popular with guests, but don't be surprised if they sample parts of it before the evening is out!

RECIPE • urn • floral foam • wire netting • reel and stub wires • wooden skewers • 3 Apples • 3 Clementines • 2 Limes
2 bunches of Grapes • 1 Mango • 3 Pomadillo • 2 Star Fruit • Kumquats • *Ranunculus* • Iceland Poppies • Roses
Violets • *Galax* leaves • assorted leaves such as Ivy, *Bergenia* or *Hosta* • *Hypericum* berries • Sycamore shoots • 3 *Protea*

1 Soak the foam and pack a block into the urn. Cut a smaller piece, place on top and insert two wooden skewers through it into the block underneath to hold it. Wrap a short length of wire netting around the foam for added security and tie to the urn with reel wire. The top piece of foam will dry out very quickly, so water will need to be drizzled in from the top to keep everything in the top section supplied with water. This display is designed really to last just one night.

2 Insert the leaves into the foam, with the largest around the rim and the others at intervals up the mound. Do not cover all the foam; they are just for the fruits to rest on. Mount the fruits onto two wooden skewers as this prevents them from turning round in the foam. Support the grapes on two skewers with stub wire. Cut some fruits in half. Add the largest fruits first, keeping these more to the base of the mound. Place them against leaves, tuck them under leaves and, in the case of cut fruit, group close together with the cut sides uppermost.

3 Keep the Violets in bunches. Push a stick up into the stems and force the bunch into the foam to get water. Tuck between the fruits. Add Roses on longer stems. Pieces close to the foam are the recessed items. Now provide the outer layer; a little more foliage will fill spaces.

4 Feature the Poppies, *Ranunculus* and *Protea* grouped in colours. Place between the fruits, making sure they are inserted into the foam. The design will become solid again so place some flowers flowing down from the container rim to lighten the edges of the arrangement.

HAPPY CHRISTMAS

Christmas tables often need 'moody' arrangements and most certainly they need candles. Whilst many arrangements made for this time of the year are made entirely with artificial materials, I prefer always to use fresh materials with maybe just a touch of something sparkly. It is not always easy to get enough fresh *Hellebore* flowers from the garden, but they are produced commercially and, although expensive, they are well worth the indulgence. They are such beautiful flowers especially when foiled by the evergreens of the Christmas season, and they last a long time. Just look on them as a Christmas treat. This arrangement is for a small table but a matching pair would be just as effective on a long table.

RECIPE • small shallow dish • floral foam • candle mounted on sticks • Noble Fir • berried Ivy • 5 or 6 small Ivy trails
2 stems of *Ilex verticillata* berries • clusters of *Cotoneaster* berries • small branches of *Garrya elliptica* • 10 *Hellebore*
flowers • 3 cones mounted on wire • 3 small glitter stars • 5 ribbon tails mounted on wire

1 Prepare the container in the usual way, soaking the foam, trimming the edges and taping to the container with anchor tape, making sure to pass the tape all the way underneath and back to stick to itself. Position the pre-mounted candle centrally. Radiate small pieces of the Noble Fir low down over the container rim with two or three pieces around the candle.

2 Intersperse the Noble Fir with the *Cotoneaster* berries and start to add a few pieces of variegated Ivy.

3 Fill in with the *Garrya elliptica* and add the Ivy trails to the lower edges. Cut up the *Ilex verticillata* and arrange low down in the design and around the candle, at the same length as the other pieces of foliage. Fill empty spaces with berried Ivy, then add the Hellebores.

4 Tuck in the cones and stars between the foliage. Arrange the ribbons radiating out from the centre but at differing angles so they do not become a frill effect. All that then remains is to light the candle.

IN THE DEEP MIDWINTER

Here is an attractive, detailed arrangement using crisp looking materials
in a mainly vegetative style, that is, the elements are arranged as they
would naturally grow. The body of the design is very low, allowing
the *Eucharis* stems to feature, standing tall and slim.

RECIPE • 4 *Eucharis* • 5 white *Nerine* flowers • lichen-covered twigs • 5 white *Euphorbia fulgens* • 7 Seminole leaves
Eucalyptus buds • 6 short stems of Privet berries • 7 white *Cyclamen* flowers • 10 *Cyclamen* leaves • 2 Ornamental
Cabbages • *Eucalyptus parvifolia* foliage • floral foam • wreath pins • terracotta saucer

1 Soak the foam and tape to the saucer. Pin the lichen branches to the foam with the wreath pins, lying them across the foam in a parallel fashion. Cut the stems of the *Eucharis* to different lengths.

2 Place the *Eucharis* vertically in the centre of the foam. To achieve the vegetative style, do not radiate the stems from the centre, but place the stems parallel to each other. Tuck the *Cyclamen* leaves in the spaces between the twigs on the two long sides and add the two cabbages above them. Cut the *Euphorbia fulgens* fairly short and place them, two on each side, horizontally and diagonally to the line of the twigs. Add the fifth at a higher level radiating from the base of the *Eucharis*. Use small pieces of *Eucalyptus* to fill spaces between the twigs.

3 Group the white *Cyclamen* flowers and white *Nerine* flowers by variety along the other diagonal – not in straight lines. Make sure the stems are cut at different lengths, varying between 4 and 7 inches (10-18cm) long.

4 Fill in with small groups of Privet berries and *Eucalyptus* buds. Take the Seminole leaves and use them horizontally to 'wrap' the design, inserting both ends into the foam. Cut both ends to a V-shape and thread them carefully into the arrangement.

CANDLESTICK DISPLAY

A candlecup is a very useful container to add to the top of a candlestick or even a bottle. The one used here was originally white, but I painted it with a small pot of special emulsion paint so that it matched the verdigris candlestick I had chosen. This combination makes an elegant footed container lifting a design when space is limited on a table. This display can stand on a dresser or sideboard, but is designed to go mid table for a meal setting. The candlestick is high enough to be able to see the person opposite underneath the bulk of the flowers. The wild Scabious featured in this arrangement were picked from a garden and not from the wild.

RECIPE • candlecup • candlestick • cylinder of foam • candle • anchor tape • cocktail sticks • Ivy trails • Clary
Rosemary • Wild Scabious • *Pittosporum* • Roses • *Spiraea* • 5 *Zantedeschia* • *Stachys* leaves • Pinks
perennial *Geranium* leaf • Lavender • *Nigella* • *Freesia*

1 Paint the candlecup, if necessary, and place on the candlestick.
Soak the cylinder of foam, trim the top edge and tape into the cup.
Mount the candle on sticks with anchor tape and place centrally in
the cylinder.

2 Make an outline of the foliages and *Nigella* buds, just as you would
for a posy in foam, but allow the trails to flow down over the
candlecup and half way down the candlestick. Turn the arrangement
round to ensure an even balance.

3 Overlay the outline material with similar length *Freesia*, Scabious
and Clary, then place the *Zantedeschia* through the centre from one
side to the other. Cut the Roses very short and tuck in deep. Fill any
gaps, at the necessary length, with Pinks and Lavender.

ANEMONE POT

Here is an easy arrangement which will suit a kitchen table
equally as well as a coffee table. The outrageously vibrant colours
look wonderful together and the open faces with their lovely
black button centres are in keeping with
the simplicity of the design.

RECIPE • terracotta half–pot • small piece of polythene • lichen moss and green moss • rough string
4 or 5 bunches of mixed *Anemone* • raffia

1 Carefully collect the *Anemone* stems in your hand, keeping them roughly parallel and vertical, and arranging the heads into a gentle dome shape. Make sure that the different colours are evenly dispersed throughout. Trim the stems level and tie tightly with raffia.

2 Line the pot with the piece of polythene. Place some green moss at the bottom and around the inside. Insert the flowers and pack more green moss around the stems until the bunch is stable. Trim off the excess polythene. Add water to the pot.

3 If the lichen moss is fresh, it may well be fairly dry and consequently brittle. If so, drop it into water and then squeeze it out. If it is preserved, it can be used without any further preparation. Tuck the grey lichen moss around the stems of the flowers.

4 Tie the rough string around the stems and wind it round and round loosely to decorate. Don't forget to drizzle a little water into the pot from time to time, taking care not to overfill, since moss has a tendency to siphon water just where it is not supposed to go.

143

TULIPAMANIA

Parrot tulips have a special quality all of their own. No matter whether they are picked from a garden or bought from a shop they are self willed and will end up doing their own thing – flopping! So my argument is to let them. By choosing a rounded container, the soft curves they fall into are repeated and the two marry together so well. You must ignore their lax habit when you arrange and just persevere. The end result is something so relaxed comfortable it is a joy to be around.

RECIPE • 1 goldfish bowl • 30 to 50 Tulips, depending on the size of the bowl

1 Fill the container with water to within a couple of inches (5cm) from the top. Arrange some Tulips around the rim, altering the length a little to produce a wavy line of heads. Trim off any excess foliage. If you leave too much on, it can be difficult to get the final stems in. Re-cut each stem as you go.

2 Continue adding more Tulips and you will find they will begin to stand up a little more. If you cross the stems to make a tracery in the water, they will act like crumpled wire netting and support subsequent additions.

3 Add all the remaining Tulips. It may begin to be difficult to push the stems through and, if so, gently rotate the stem back and forth. This will make it easier. Once you have the last one in, stand back and enjoy the magnificent display.

SIMPLE ROSES

I do not believe I have met anyone who does not enjoy the sight of a bowl of garden Roses. The Rose here is one I love. 'Margaret Merril' is often classed as a white Rose but as it develops, it becomes gently flushed with the palest of shell pink overtones. However, it's best characteristic must be the perfume, a heady old-fashioned Rose scent. Used on a dining table with a silver container, it gives distinction to any setting, pervading the room both with the perfume and its simple elegance. Of course there are other Roses which have similar qualities, but this one is magnificent. The arrangement here was placed on a small table covered with tulle, a good idea for dressing a table for a wedding breakfast.

RECIPE • silver dish with small foot • floral foam • piece of polythene • anchor tape (optional)
20 stems of garden Roses • 10 or 12 short Ivy trails and a few larger Ivy leaves

1 Line the dish with polythene to protect it. Soak the foam, trim the top edges and shape the bottom to fit the container. Fit securely using tape if necessary. The Roses being used are not too heavy and so it is unlikely, as long as the piece of foam fits snugly, that you will need to do anything further.

2 Begin as always with the outline, using the Ivy trails flowing over the rim, establishing a gentle curved top profile and an oval shape. Cover some of the exposed foam with two or three extra Ivy leaves.

3 Start with the smallest Roses, or those most in bud. Keeping within the Ivy framework, arrange the Roses into an oval, altering the angle each time creating slight undulation. Now add two or three Roses higher up in the design but still within the outline.

4 Fill in with the remaining Roses, cutting some quite short and sinking them deeper into the design. Remove foliage from the stems as necessary, adding it separately to hide any foam left showing. Fill in with Ivy leaves if the Rose foliage is not good enough.

PLANT
DIRECTORY

THIS DIRECTORY contains some of the materials I use most often in my floral work. It is by no means a comprehensive directory of all the different flowers and foliages you could use: that would have filled the whole book and more. Don't limit your arrangements to the materials you find here; it is merely meant as a guide to demonstrate the sheer range of what is available. Be experimental and try out whatever you find in the florist or the garden.

KEY TO SYMBOLS

Availability
The times of year shown are the times when the particular material is available from any source – a florist or a garden. Nowadays, much material is grown commercially and is available outside its natural garden season.

Conditioning (see page 38 for further details)
① Deep, cold water treatment
② Hot or warm water treatment
③ Shallow cold water treatment
④ Singe the cut ends of the stems with a match
❀ Use cut flower food

Fragrance
☆ denotes the plant is fragrant or aromatic.

Preserving (see page 42 for further details)
❶ Air dry
❷ Preserve with glycerine
❸ Preserve with a desiccant
❹ Dry flat, pressed between layers of newspaper

Vase life
The following symbols denote the length of time a flower or piece of foliage should last in a display, under normal conditions with the correct conditioning:
◖ under one week
◖◖ one week to ten days
◖◖◖ over ten days

Danger
◆ denotes the plant is either poisonous or liable to cause an allergic reaction.

Abies procera
Blue Fir – Blue Pine – Noble Fir
Foliage (all year) ① ○○○ ☆

Acacia
Mimosa – Wattle
Flowers (autumn-spring) ① ❸ ○ ☆ ✿

Acer pseudoplatanus
Sycamore
Foliage (early sping) Seedheads (summer) ② ❶ ○

Achillea
Yarrow
Flowers (summer) ① ❶ ○○○

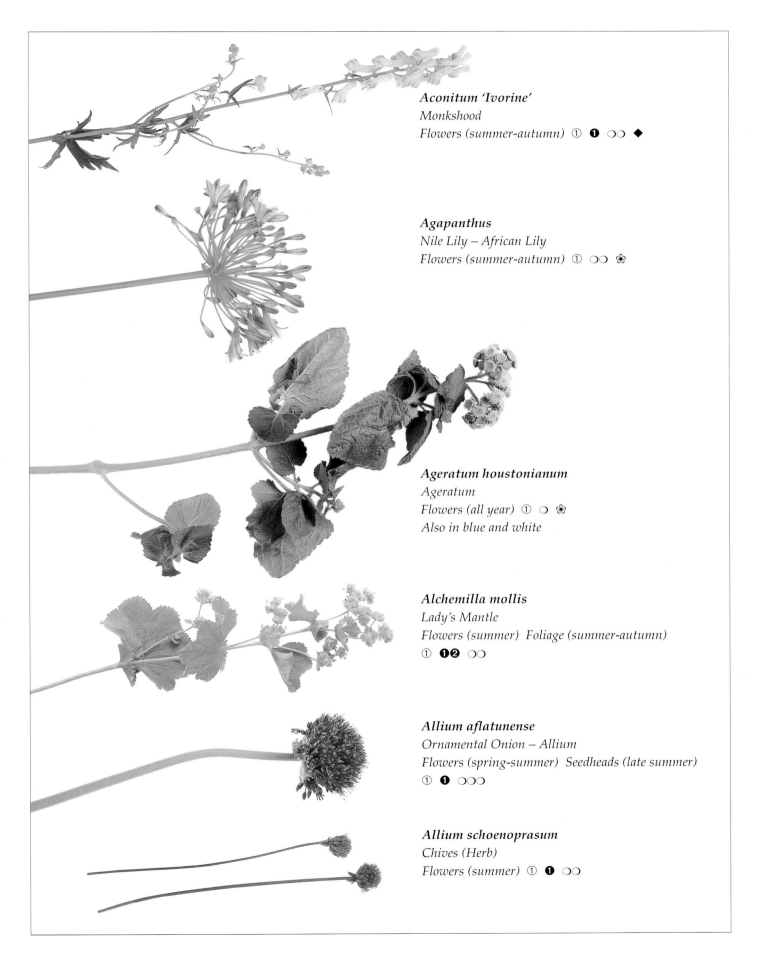

Aconitum 'Ivorine'
Monkshood
Flowers (summer-autumn) ① ❶ ◯◯ ◆

Agapanthus
Nile Lily – African Lily
Flowers (summer-autumn) ① ◯◯ ✽

Ageratum houstonianum
Ageratum
Flowers (all year) ① ◯ ✽
Also in blue and white

Alchemilla mollis
Lady's Mantle
Flowers (summer) Foliage (summer-autumn)
① ❶❷ ◯◯

Allium aflatunense
Ornamental Onion – Allium
Flowers (spring-summer) Seedheads (late summer)
① ❶ ◯◯◯

Allium schoenoprasum
Chives (Herb)
Flowers (summer) ① ❶ ◯◯

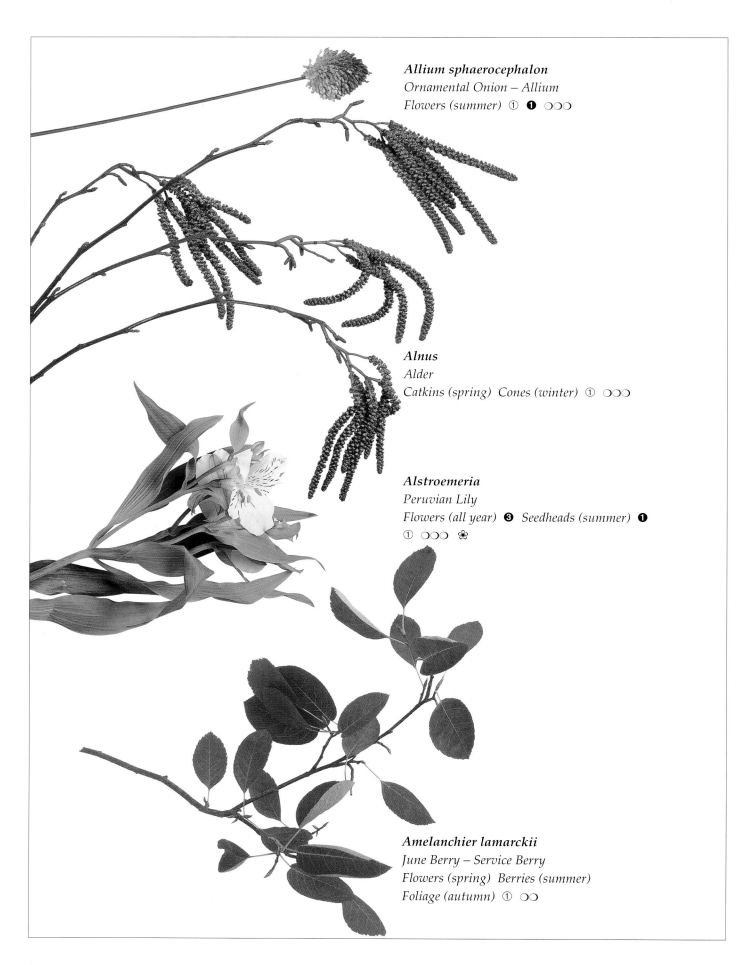

Allium sphaerocephalon
Ornamental Onion – Allium
Flowers (summer) ① ❶ ○○○

Alnus
Alder
Catkins (spring) Cones (winter) ① ○○○

Alstroemeria
Peruvian Lily
Flowers (all year) ❸ *Seedheads (summer)* ❶
① ○○○ ✿

Amelanchier lamarckii
June Berry – Service Berry
Flowers (spring) Berries (summer)
Foliage (autumn) ① ○○

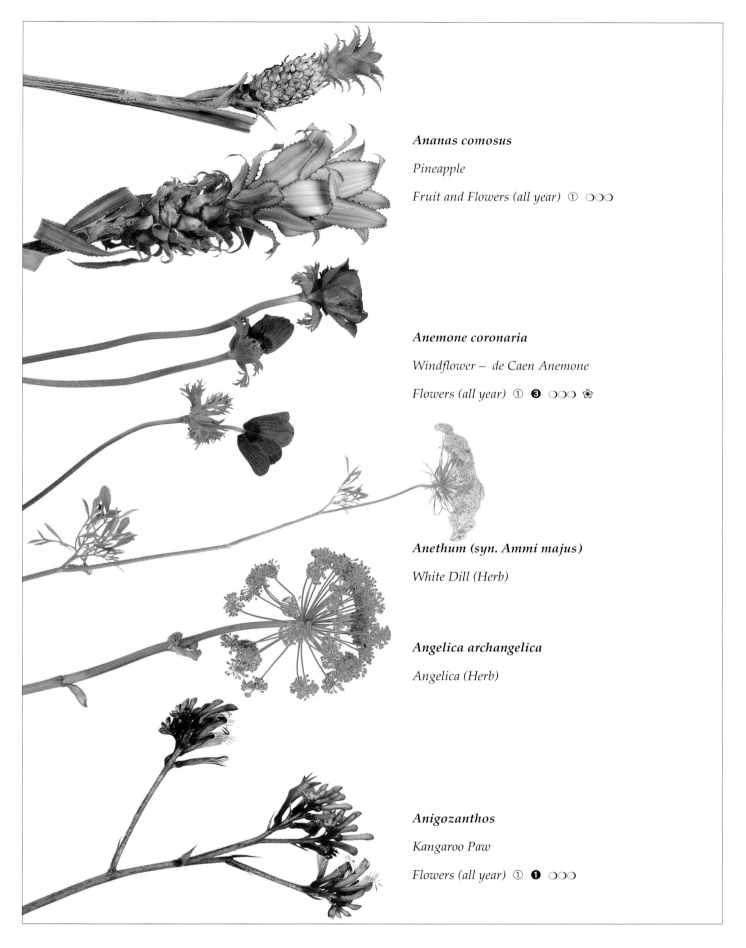

Ananas comosus

Pineapple

Fruit and Flowers (all year) ① ○○○

Anemone coronaria

Windflower – de Caen Anemone

Flowers (all year) ① ❸ ○○○ ✿

Anethum (syn. Ammi majus)

White Dill (Herb)

Angelica archangelica

Angelica (Herb)

Anigozanthos

Kangaroo Paw

Flowers (all year) ① ❶ ○○○

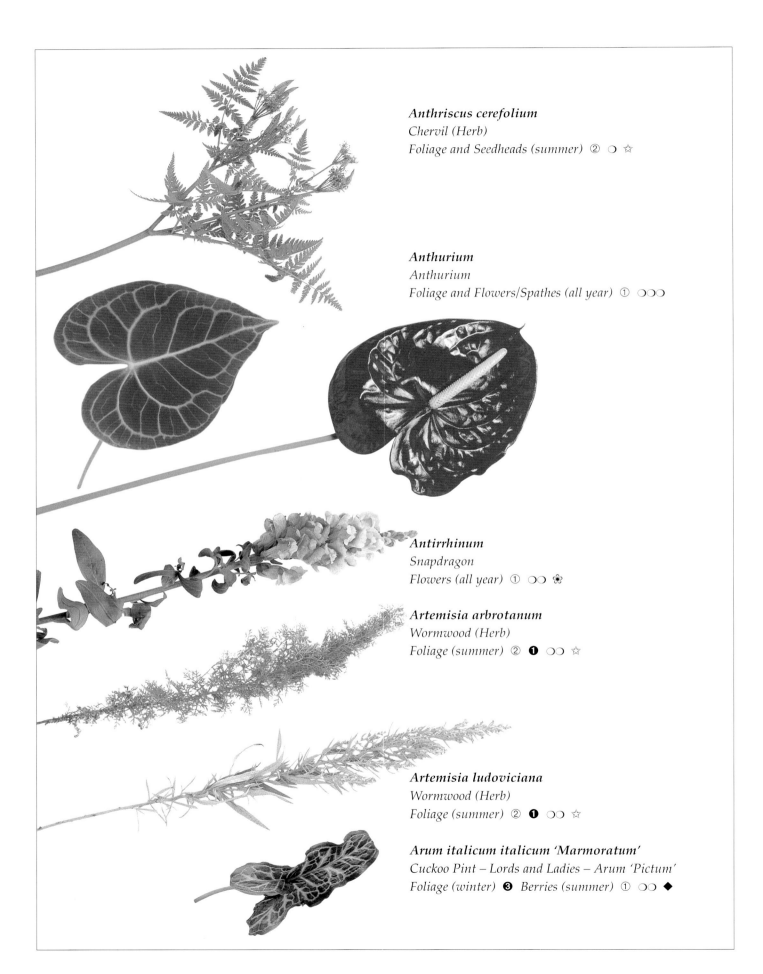

Anthriscus cerefolium
Chervil (Herb)
Foliage and Seedheads (summer) ② ○ ☆

Anthurium
Anthurium
Foliage and Flowers/Spathes (all year) ① ○○○

Antirrhinum
Snapdragon
Flowers (all year) ① ○○ ✿

Artemisia arbrotanum
Wormwood (Herb)
Foliage (summer) ② ❶ ○○ ☆

Artemisia ludoviciana
Wormwood (Herb)
Foliage (summer) ② ❶ ○○ ☆

Arum italicum italicum 'Marmoratum'
Cuckoo Pint – Lords and Ladies – Arum 'Pictum'
Foliage (winter) ❸ Berries (summer) ① ○○ ◆

Asparagus densiflorus Sprengeri
Asparagus – Sprengeri
Foliage (all year) ① ❷ ○

Aspidistra
Aspidistra
Foliage (all year) ① ❷ ○○○

Aster
Michaelmas Daisy – September Flower
Flowers (all year) ① ❸ ○ ✿

Astilbe
False Spiraea
Flowers and Seedheads (summer) ① ❶ ○ ✿

Astrantia major
Masterwort
Flowers (summer) ② ❸ ○○ ✿

Berberis thunbergii atropurpurea
Barberry
Foliage (spring-autumn) Berries (autumn) ② ○○

Bergenia cordifolia
Elephant's Ears
Foliage (all year) Flowers (spring) ① ○○○

Calendula officinalis
Pot Marigold (Herb)
Flowers (spring-autumn) ① ❸ ○○ ✽

Calluna
Heather – Scotch Heather
Flowers (summer-autumn) ① ❶ ○○

Camellia
Camellia
Foliage (all year) ○○○ *Flowers (spring)* ○ ① ❷

Campanula
Bellflower
Flowers (summer) ① ❸ ○○ ✾

Capsicum annuum
Cherry Pepper
Fruits (autumn-winter) ① ❶ ○○○

Celosia
Cock's Comb
Flowers (autumn-winter) ① ❶❸ ○○○ ✾

Centaurea cyanus
Cornflower
Flowers (summer-autumn) ① ❶❸ ○○
More commonly in blue or white

Centaurea montana
Perennial Cornflower
Flowers (summer) ① ○ ✾

Centaurea moschata
Sweet Sultan
Flowers (summer) ① ❸ ○○

Centranthus ruber
Valerian
Flowers (summer) ① ○○

Chrysanthemum 'Ping Pong'
Pompom Chrysanthemum (syn. Dendranthema)
Flowers (all year) ① ❸ ○○

Chrysanthemum 'Shamrock'
Spider Chrysanthemum (syn. Dendranthema)
Flowers (all year) ① ❸ ○○

Chrysanthemum
Spray Chrysanthemum (syn. Dendranthema)
Flowers (all year) ① ❸ ○○

Cirsium rivulare atropurpureum
Plume Thistle
Flowers (summer) ② ❸ ○○ ✿

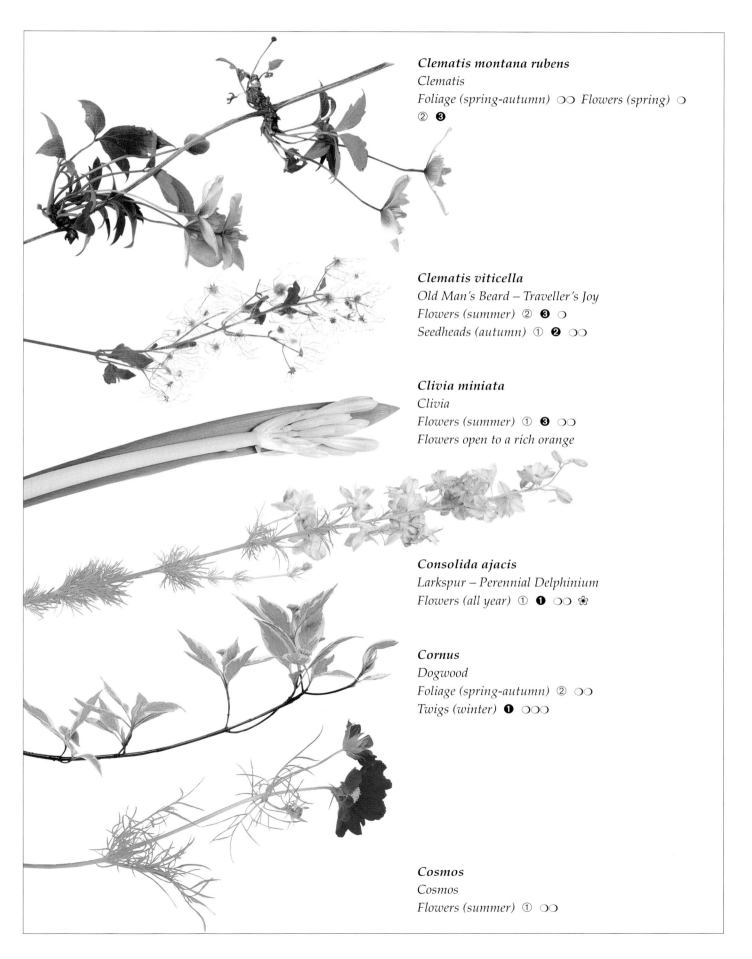

Clematis montana rubens
Clematis
Foliage (spring-autumn) ○○ *Flowers (spring)* ○
② ❸

Clematis viticella
Old Man's Beard – Traveller's Joy
Flowers (summer) ② ❸ ○
Seedheads (autumn) ① ❷ ○○

Clivia miniata
Clivia
Flowers (summer) ① ❸ ○○
Flowers open to a rich orange

Consolida ajacis
Larkspur – Perennial Delphinium
Flowers (all year) ① ❶ ○○ ✿

Cornus
Dogwood
Foliage (spring-autumn) ② ○○
Twigs (winter) ❶ ○○○

Cosmos
Cosmos
Flowers (summer) ① ○○

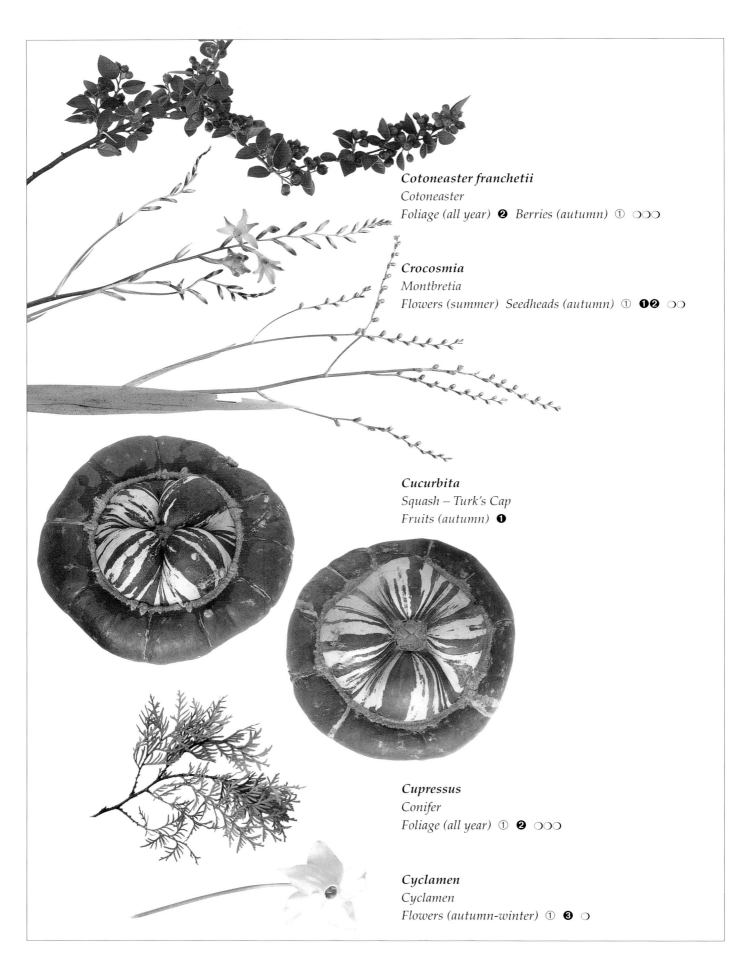

Cotoneaster franchetii
Cotoneaster
Foliage (all year) ❷ *Berries (autumn)* ① ○○○

Crocosmia
Montbretia
Flowers (summer) Seedheads (autumn) ① ❶❷ ○○

Cucurbita
Squash – Turk's Cap
Fruits (autumn) ❶

Cupressus
Conifer
Foliage (all year) ① ❷ ○○○

Cyclamen
Cyclamen
Flowers (autumn-winter) ① ❸ ○

Cyclamen
Cyclamen leaves
Foliage (autumn-winter) ① ○○

Cynara cardunculus
Artichoke
Foliage (spring-autumn) ○ *Flowers (summer)* ○○
Seedheads (autumn) ○○ ② ❶

Cytisus
Broom
Flowers (spring) ○ *Foliage (summer-winter)* ○○
① ☆ ✿

Dahlia
Dahlia
Flowers (autumn) ① ❸ ○ ✿ (❶ *pompom varieties*)

Delphinium
Delphinium
Flowers (spring-autumn) Seedheads (autumn)
② ❶❸ ○ ✿

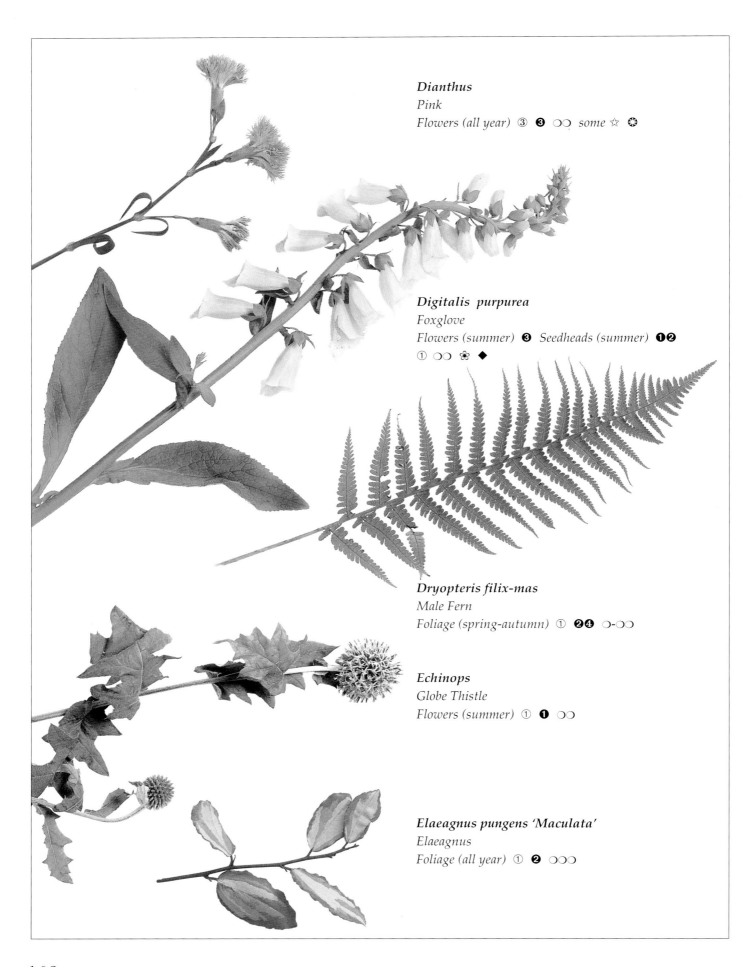

Dianthus
Pink
Flowers (all year) ③ ❸ ○○ some ☆ ✸

Digitalis purpurea
Foxglove
Flowers (summer) ❸ Seedheads (summer) ❶❷
① ○○ ✸ ◆

Dryopteris filix-mas
Male Fern
Foliage (spring-autumn) ① ❷❹ ○-○○

Echinops
Globe Thistle
Flowers (summer) ① ❶ ○○

Elaeagnus pungens 'Maculata'
Elaeagnus
Foliage (all year) ① ❷ ○○○

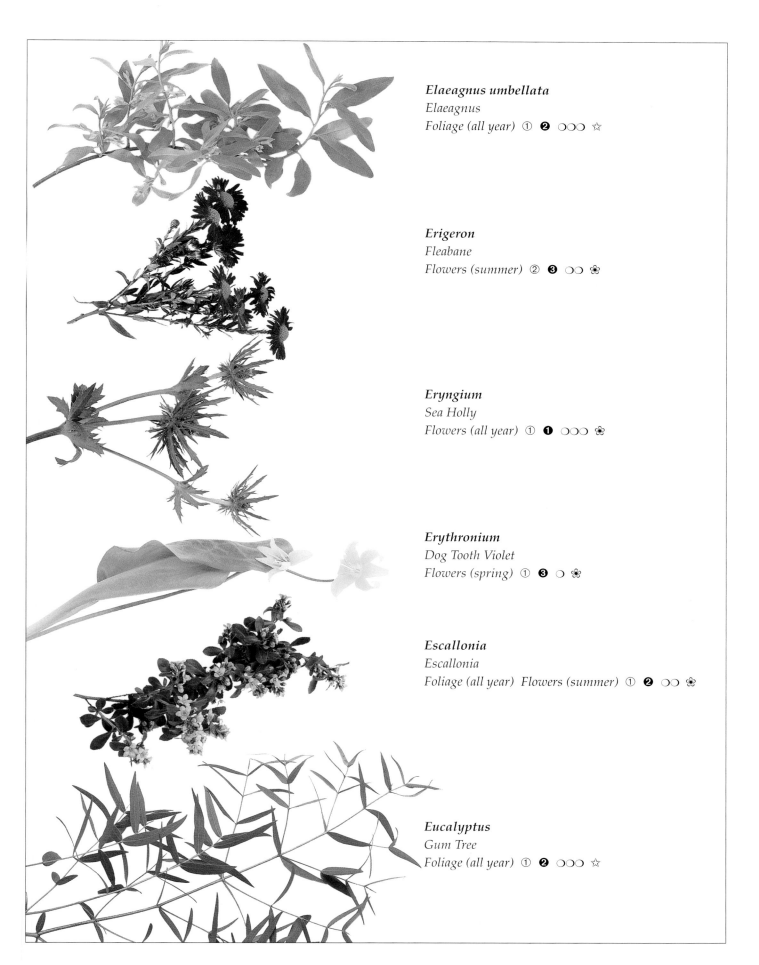

Elaeagnus umbellata
Elaeagnus
Foliage (all year) ① ❷ ○○○ ☆

Erigeron
Fleabane
Flowers (summer) ② ❸ ○○ ✿

Eryngium
Sea Holly
Flowers (all year) ① ❶ ○○○ ✿

Erythronium
Dog Tooth Violet
Flowers (spring) ① ❸ ○ ✿

Escallonia
Escallonia
Foliage (all year) Flowers (summer) ① ❷ ○○ ✿

Eucalyptus
Gum Tree
Foliage (all year) ① ❷ ○○○ ☆

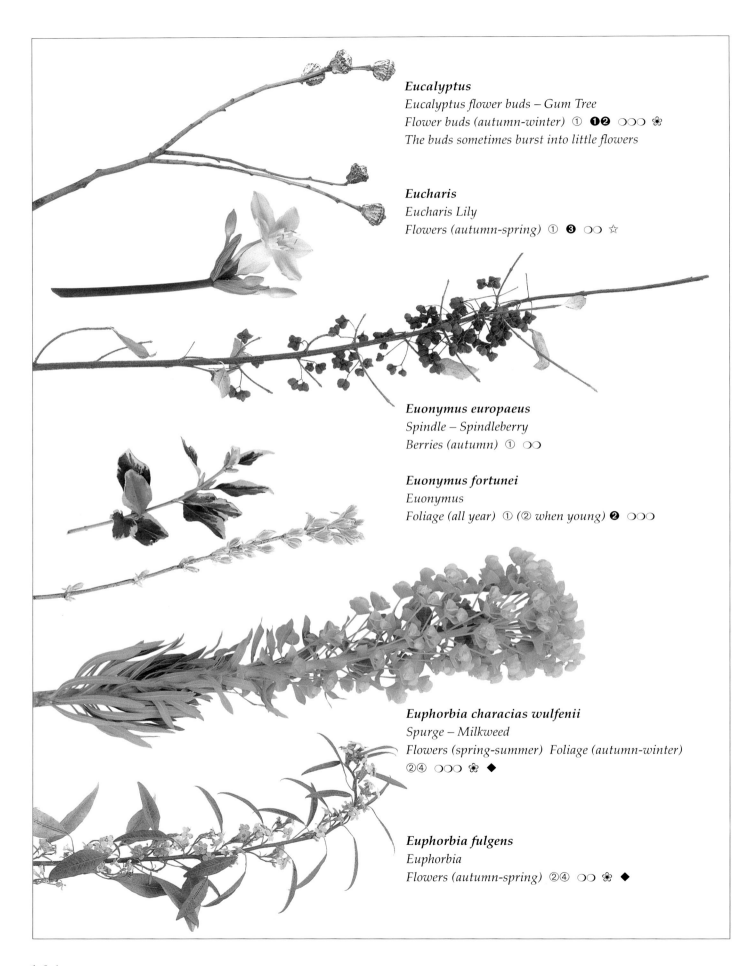

Eucalyptus
Eucalyptus flower buds – Gum Tree
Flower buds (autumn-winter) ① ❶❷ ○○○ ❀
The buds sometimes burst into little flowers

Eucharis
Eucharis Lily
Flowers (autumn-spring) ① ❸ ○○ ☆

Euonymus europaeus
Spindle – Spindleberry
Berries (autumn) ① ○○

Euonymus fortunei
Euonymus
Foliage (all year) ① (② when young) ❷ ○○○

Euphorbia characias wulfenii
Spurge – Milkweed
Flowers (spring-summer) Foliage (autumn-winter)
②④ ○○○ ❀ ◆

Euphorbia fulgens
Euphorbia
Flowers (autumn-spring) ②④ ○○ ❀ ◆

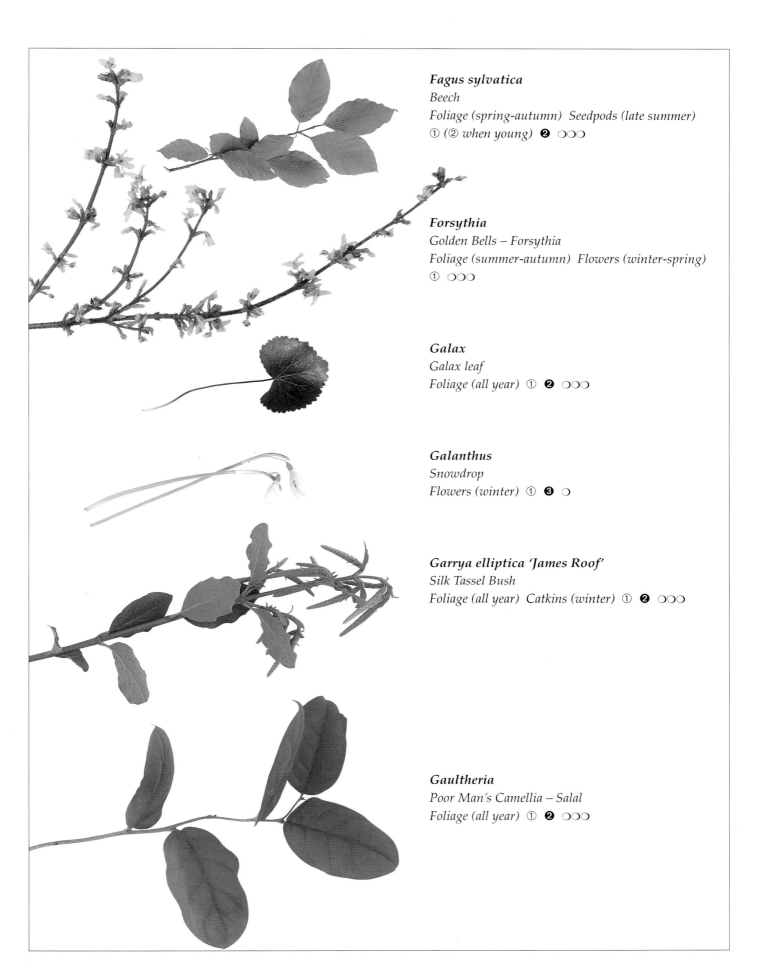

Fagus sylvatica
Beech
Foliage (spring–autumn) Seedpods (late summer)
① (② *when young*) ❷ ○○○

Forsythia
Golden Bells – Forsythia
Foliage (summer–autumn) Flowers (winter–spring)
① ○○○

Galax
Galax leaf
Foliage (all year) ① ❷ ○○○

Galanthus
Snowdrop
Flowers (winter) ① ❸ ○

Garrya elliptica 'James Roof'
Silk Tassel Bush
Foliage (all year) Catkins (winter) ① ❷ ○○○

Gaultheria
Poor Man's Camellia – Salal
Foliage (all year) ① ❷ ○○○

Gerbera jamesonii
Transvaal Daisy
Flowers (all year) ③ ❸ ○○○ ❀

Gomphocarpus physocarpus
Silkweed
Seed cases (autumn-winter) ② ❹ ○○○ ❀ ◆

Gomphrena
Globe Amaranth
Flowers (all year) ② ❶ ○○ ❀

Hebe
Veronica
Flowers and foliage (all year) ② ❷ ○○ ❀
Herbaceous Veronica illustrated

Hedera canariensis
Ivy
Foliage (all year) ① ❷❸ ○○○ ◆

Hedera helix
Ivy
Foliage (all year) ① ❷❸ ○○○ ◆

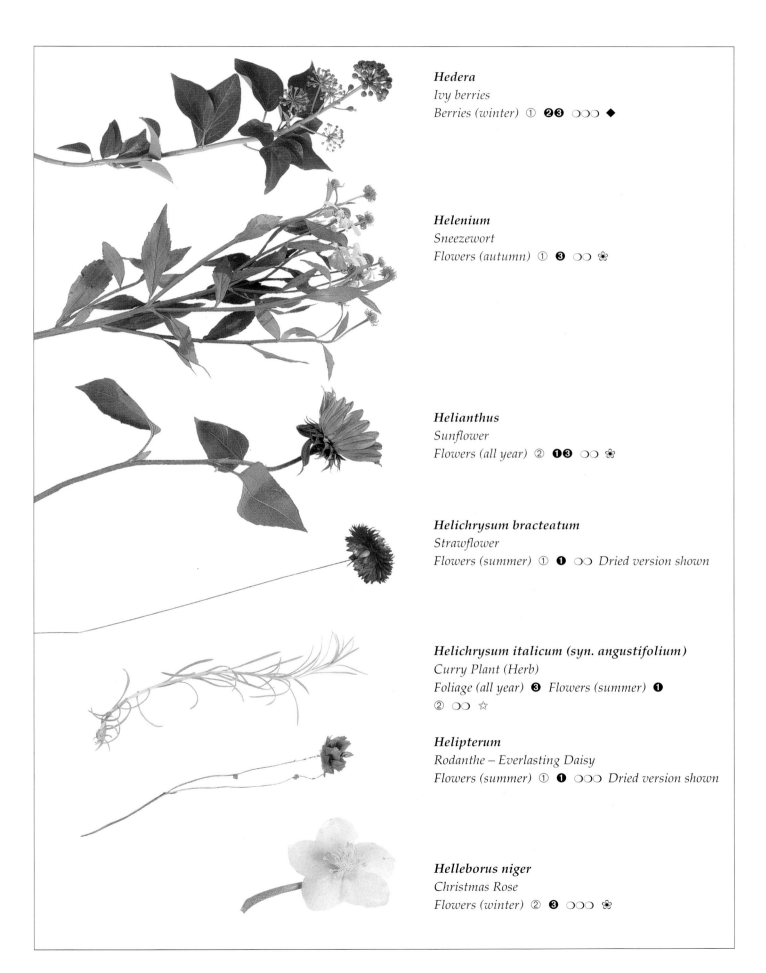

Hedera
Ivy berries
Berries (winter) ① ❷❸ ○○○ ◆

Helenium
Sneezewort
Flowers (autumn) ① ❸ ○○ ✿

Helianthus
Sunflower
Flowers (all year) ② ❶❸ ○○ ✿

Helichrysum bracteatum
Strawflower
Flowers (summer) ① ❶ ○○ *Dried version shown*

Helichrysum italicum (syn. angustifolium)
Curry Plant (Herb)
Foliage (all year) ❸ *Flowers (summer)* ❶
② ○○ ☆

Helipterum
Rodanthe – Everlasting Daisy
Flowers (summer) ① ❶ ○○○ *Dried version shown*

Helleborus niger
Christmas Rose
Flowers (winter) ② ❸ ○○○ ✿

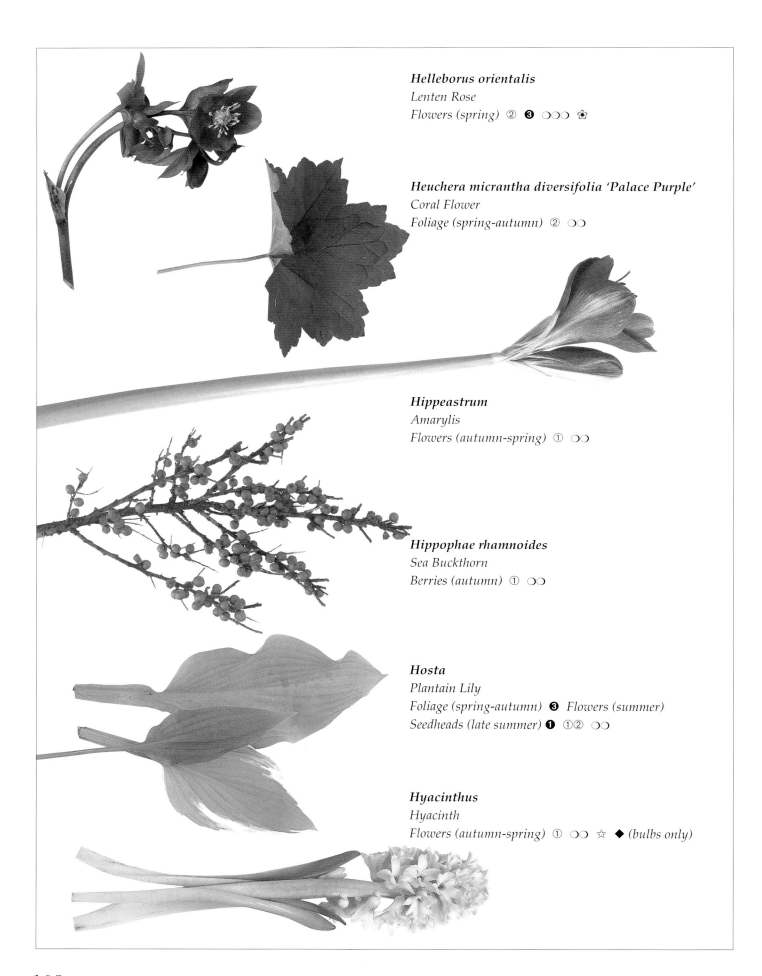

Helleborus orientalis
Lenten Rose
Flowers (spring) ② ❸ ○○○ ✿

Heuchera micrantha diversifolia 'Palace Purple'
Coral Flower
Foliage (spring-autumn) ② ○○

Hippeastrum
Amarylis
Flowers (autumn-spring) ① ○○

Hippophae rhamnoides
Sea Buckthorn
Berries (autumn) ① ○○

Hosta
Plantain Lily
Foliage (spring-autumn) ❸ *Flowers (summer)*
Seedheads (late summer) ❶ ①② ○○

Hyacinthus
Hyacinth
Flowers (autumn-spring) ① ○○ ☆ ◆ *(bulbs only)*

Hydrangea
Hydrangea
Flowers (all year) ① (② *when young*) ❶❷ ○○-○○○

Hypericum berries
St John's Wort
Berries (all year) ① ○○

Ilex verticillata
Holly
Berries (winter) Foliage (all year) ① ○○○

Iris foetidissima
Stinking Iris – Gladdon
Foliage (all year) Berries (winter) ① ❶ ○○○

Iris sibirica
Iris
Flowers (summer) ❸ *Seedheads (autumn)* ❶ ① ○

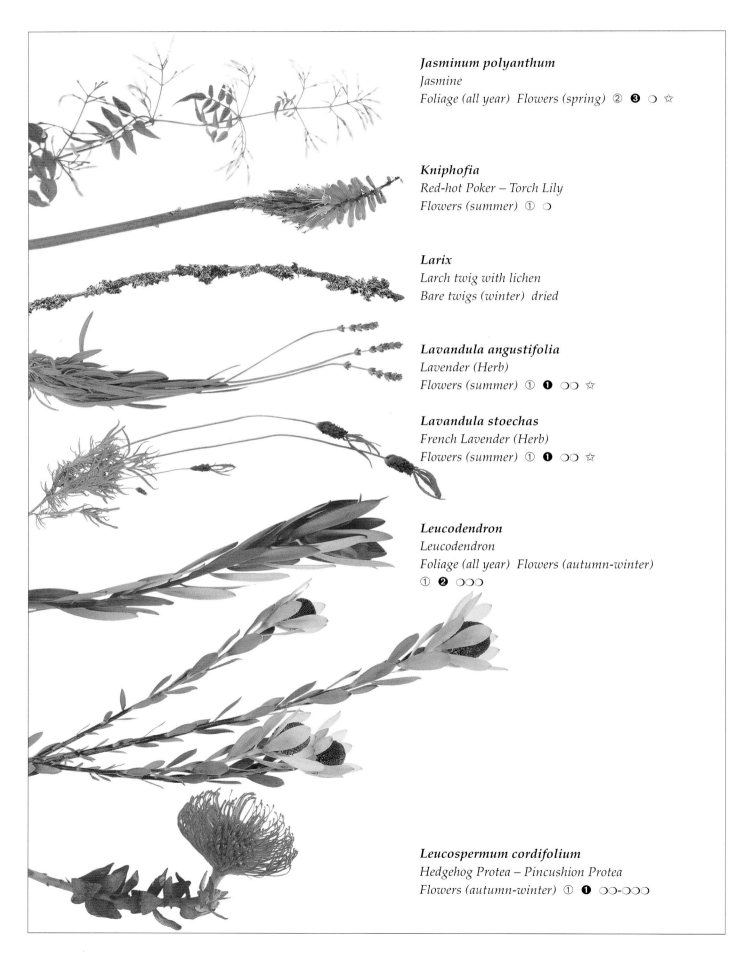

Jasminum polyanthum
Jasmine
Foliage (all year) Flowers (spring) ② ❸ ○ ☆

Kniphofia
Red-hot Poker – Torch Lily
Flowers (summer) ① ○

Larix
Larch twig with lichen
Bare twigs (winter) dried

Lavandula angustifolia
Lavender (Herb)
Flowers (summer) ① ❶ ○○ ☆

Lavandula stoechas
French Lavender (Herb)
Flowers (summer) ① ❶ ○○ ☆

Leucodendron
Leucodendron
Foliage (all year) Flowers (autumn-winter)
① ❷ ○○○

Leucospermum cordifolium
Hedgehog Protea – Pincushion Protea
Flowers (autumn-winter) ① ❶ ○○-○○○

Ligustrum
Privet – Golden Privet
Foliage (all year) ① ◯◯

Ligustrum berries
Privet berries
Berries (autumn) ① ◯◯

Lilium
Lily (Àsiatic hybrid)
Flowers (all year) ① ❸ ◯◯-◯◯◯ ✽

Lilium longiflorum
Lily
Flowers (all year) ① ❸ ◯◯-◯◯◯ ☆ ✽

Lilium regale
Lily
Flowers (all year) ① ❸ ◯◯-◯◯◯ ☆ ✿

Lilium 'Star Gazer'
Lily
Flowers (all year) ① ❸ ◯◯-◯◯◯ ☆ ✿

Limonium
Sea Lavender
Flowers (all year) ① ❶ ◯◯◯
Fresh and dried shown

Limonium sinuatum
Statice
Flowers (all year) ① ❶ ◯◯◯

Liriodendron tulipifera
Tulip Tree
Foliage and Flowers (summer) ② ❸ ◯

Lonicera
Honeysuckle
Foliage (spring-autumn) Flowers (summer-autumn)
① ❸ ○ ☆ ✽

Lonicera
Honeysuckle berries
Berries (summer-autumn) ① ○○

Lupinus
Lupin
Flowers (summer) ② ○ ✽

Lysimachia clethroides
Lysimachia
Flowers (nearly all year) ② ○○ ✽

Magnolia sieboldii sinensis
Magnolia
Foliage (all year) ① ❷ ○○○ *Flowers (spring)* ② ❸ ○○
Seedheads (summer) ① ❶ ○○○

Mahonia aquifolium
Oregon Grape
Foliage (all year) ❷ *Flowers (spring)*
Berries (autumn) ① ○○○ ☆

Malus 'Golden Hornet'
Crab Apple
Fruits (autumn) ① ○○○

Malus
Crab Apple blossom
Flowers (spring) ① ○

Matthiola incana
Stock – Brompton Stock
Flowers (spring) ① ○ ☆

Melissa officinalis
Lemon Balm (Herb)
Foliage (summer) ② ○ ☆

Mentha spicata
Mint (Herb)
Foliage (summer) ② ○ ☆

Monarda
Bergamot
Flowers (summer) ② ○○ ☆

Monstera deliciosa
Cheese Plant – Swiss Cheese Plant
Foliage (all year) ① ○○○

Muscari
Grape Hyacinth
Flowers (spring) ① ❸ ○

Narcissus hybrids
Daffodil – Narcissus
Flowers (spring) ① ❸ ○

Narcissus 'Soleil d'Or'
Narcissus
Flowers (spring) ① ❸ ○

Nepeta
Catmint (Herb)
Flowers (spring) ① ❶ ○○

Nerine bowdenii
Nerine – Guernsey Lily
Flowers (all year) ① ❸ ○○

Nerine species
Nerine
Flowers (autumn) ① ❸ ○○

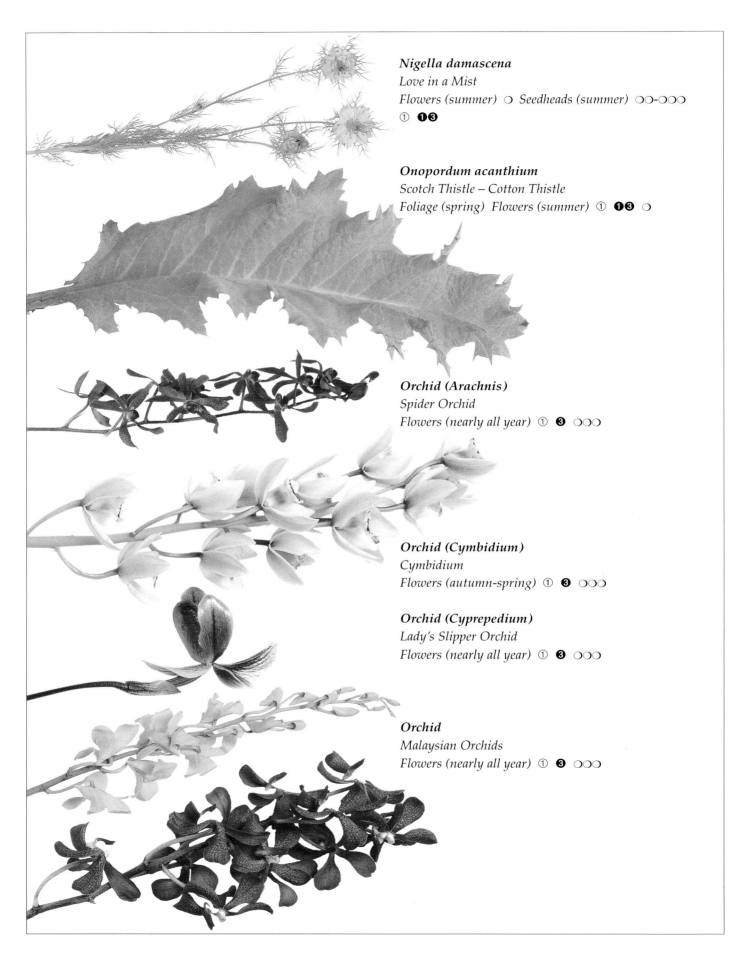

Nigella damascena
Love in a Mist
Flowers (summer) ○ *Seedheads (summer)* ○○-○○○
① ❶❸

Onopordum acanthium
Scotch Thistle – Cotton Thistle
Foliage (spring) Flowers (summer) ① ❶❸ ○

Orchid (Arachnis)
Spider Orchid
Flowers (nearly all year) ① ❸ ○○○

Orchid (Cymbidium)
Cymbidium
Flowers (autumn-spring) ① ❸ ○○○

Orchid (Cyprepedium)
Lady's Slipper Orchid
Flowers (nearly all year) ① ❸ ○○○

Orchid
Malaysian Orchids
Flowers (nearly all year) ① ❸ ○○○

Ornithogalum arabicum
Chincherinchee – Star of Bethlehem
Flowers (all year) ① ○○○

Ornithogalum thyrsoides
Chincherinchee
Flowers (all year) ① ○○○

Osmanthus
Osmanthus
Foliage (all year) Flowers (spring) ① ❷ ○○○ ☆

Paeonia
Tree Peony
Foliage (spring-autumn) ❷ *Flowers (summer)* ❸
Seedheads (autumn) ❶ ① ○○

Paeonia lactiflora
Peony
Flowers (summer) ① ❸ ○○ ✿

Paeonia lactiflora 'Sarah Bernhardt'
Peony
Flowers (summer) ① ❸ ○○○ ✿

Papaver nudicaule
Iceland Poppy
Flowers (spring-summer) ②③④ ❸ ○○ ✿

Parthenocissus
Boston Ivy – Virginia Creeper (depending on species)
Foliage (summer-autumn) ① ○-○○

Penstemon 'Sour Grapes'
Penstemon
Flowers (summer) ② ❸ ○○ ✿

Petroselinum crispum
Parsley (Herb)
Foliage (spring-autumn) ○ *Flowers (summer)* ○○
① ☆

Philadelphus
Mock Orange
Flowers (summer) ② ○○ ☆
Remove foliage to allow the flowers to develop

Phlox
Phlox
Flowers (summer) ① ○○ ☆ ✿

Phoenix dactylifera
Date
Buds (spring) ① ❶ ○○

Photinia x fraseri 'Red Robin'
Photinia
Foliage (nearly all year) ② ❷ ○○-○○○

Physalis
Cape Gooseberry – Chinese Lantern
Seedheads (autumn) ① ❶ ○○○

Pieris
Pieris
Foliage (all year) Flowers (spring) ① ❷ ○○○

Pittosporum
Pittosporum
Foliage (all year) ① ❷ ○○○

Polemonium caeruleum
Jacob's Ladder
Flowers (summer) ② ○○ ✤

Polygonatum
Solomon's Seal
Foliage and Flowers (spring to summer)
① (② when young) ❷ ○○○

Protea pityphylla
Red Protea
Flowers (spring) ① ❶ ○○-○○○

Protea (Leucospermum)
Hedgehog Protea – Pincushion Protea
Flowers (autumn-winter) ① ❶ ○○-○○○

Protea
King Protea
Flowers (autumn-spring) ① ❶ ○○-○○○

Prunus dulcis
Almond blossom
Flowers (spring) ① ○○

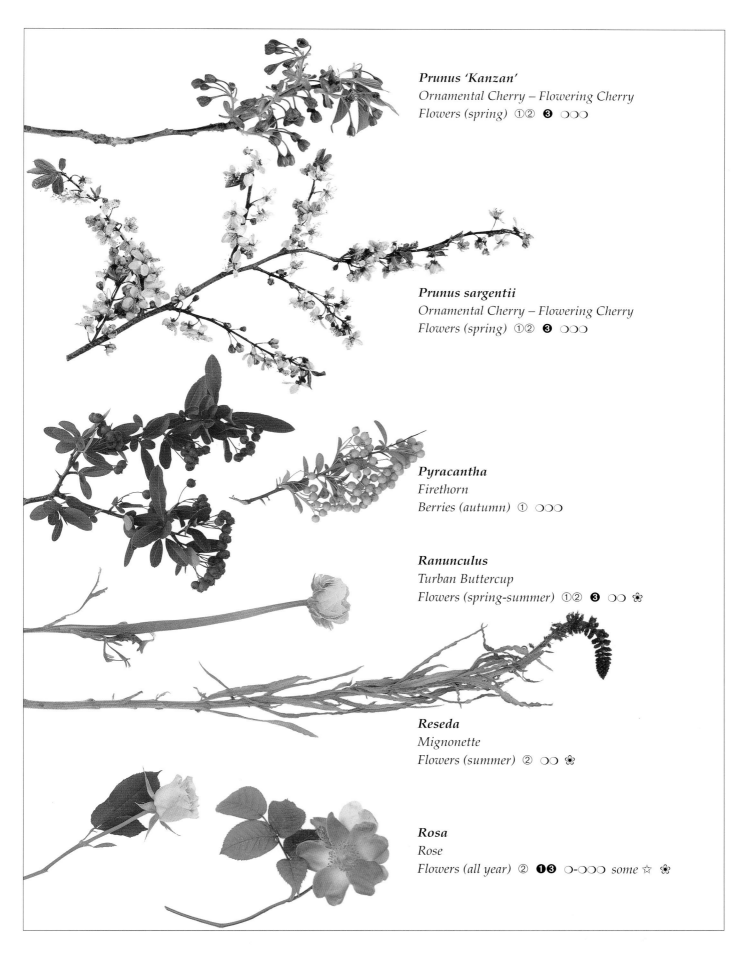

Prunus 'Kanzan'
Ornamental Cherry – Flowering Cherry
Flowers (spring) ①② ❸ ○○○

Prunus sargentii
Ornamental Cherry – Flowering Cherry
Flowers (spring) ①② ❸ ○○○

Pyracantha
Firethorn
Berries (autumn) ① ○○○

Ranunculus
Turban Buttercup
Flowers (spring-summer) ①② ❸ ○○ ❀

Reseda
Mignonette
Flowers (summer) ② ○○ ❀

Rosa
Rose
Flowers (all year) ② ❶❸ ○-○○○ *some* ☆ ❀

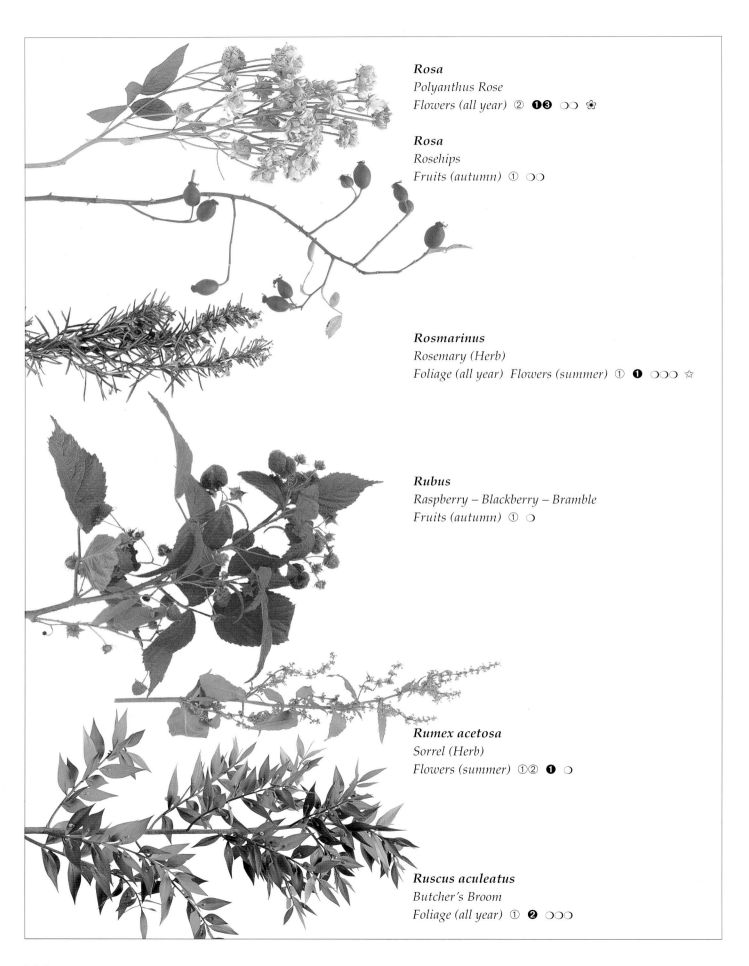

Rosa
Polyanthus Rose
Flowers (all year) ② ❶❸ ○○ ✿

Rosa
Rosehips
Fruits (autumn) ① ○○

Rosmarinus
Rosemary (Herb)
Foliage (all year) Flowers (summer) ① ❶ ○○○ ☆

Rubus
Raspberry – Blackberry – Bramble
Fruits (autumn) ① ○

Rumex acetosa
Sorrel (Herb)
Flowers (summer) ①② ❶ ○

Ruscus aculeatus
Butcher's Broom
Foliage (all year) ① ❷ ○○○

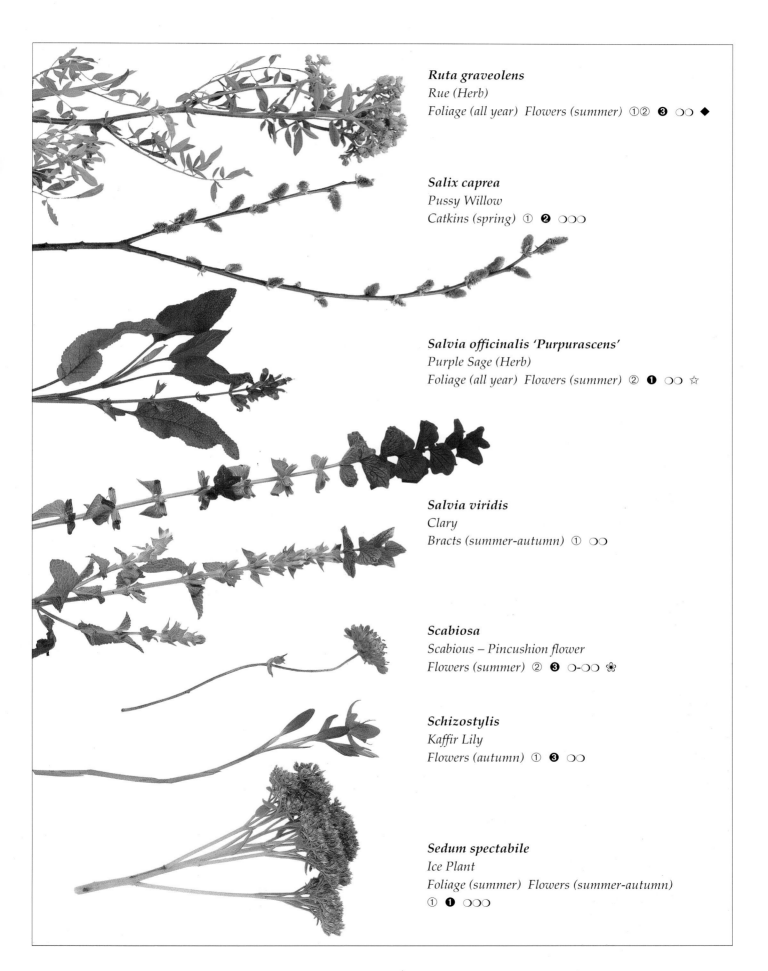

Ruta graveolens
Rue (Herb)
Foliage (all year) Flowers (summer) ①② ❸ ○○ ◆

Salix caprea
Pussy Willow
Catkins (spring) ① ❷ ○○○

Salvia officinalis 'Purpurascens'
Purple Sage (Herb)
Foliage (all year) Flowers (summer) ② ❶ ○○ ☆

Salvia viridis
Clary
Bracts (summer-autumn) ① ○○

Scabiosa
Scabious – Pincushion flower
Flowers (summer) ② ❸ ○-○○ ✿

Schizostylis
Kaffir Lily
Flowers (autumn) ① ❸ ○○

Sedum spectabile
Ice Plant
Foliage (summer) Flowers (summer-autumn)
① ❶ ○○○

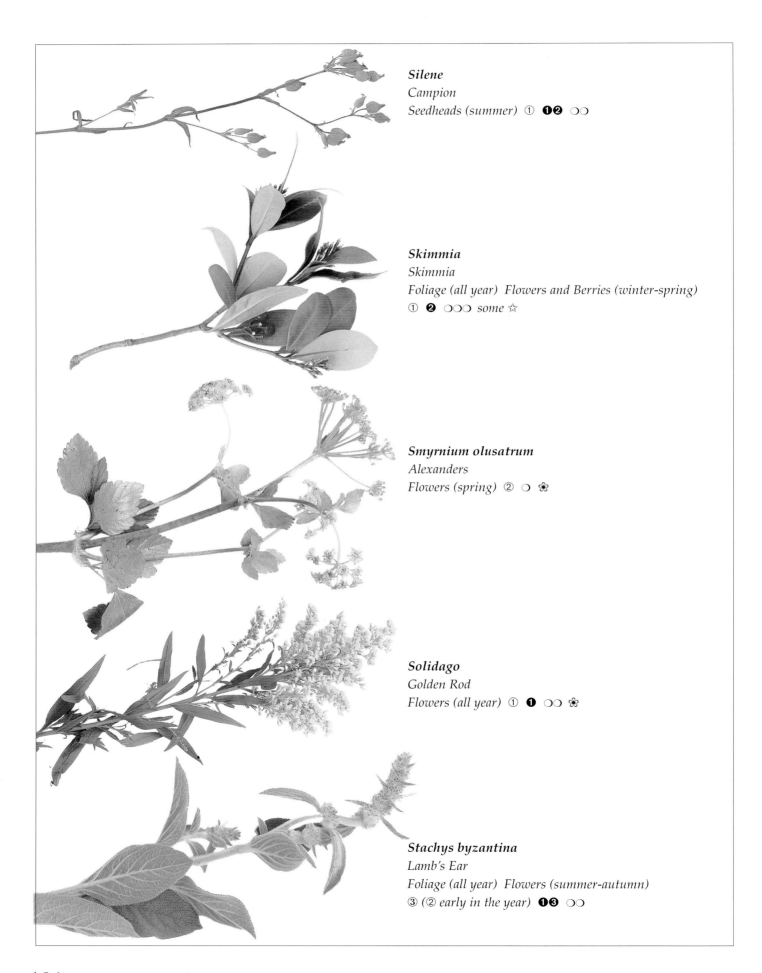

Silene
Campion
Seedheads (summer) ① ❶❷ ○○

Skimmia
Skimmia
Foliage (all year) Flowers and Berries (winter-spring)
① ❷ ○○○ some ☆

Smyrnium olusatrum
Alexanders
Flowers (spring) ② ○ ✿

Solidago
Golden Rod
Flowers (all year) ① ❶ ○○ ✿

Stachys byzantina
Lamb's Ear
Foliage (all year) Flowers (summer-autumn)
③ (② early in the year) ❶❸ ○○

Strelitzia reginae
Bird of Paradise
Foliage and Flowers (all year) ① ○○○ ✿

Symphoricarpos albus
Snowberry
Berries (summer-autumn) ① ○○

Syringa
Lilac
Flowers (winter-summer) ② ❸ ○○ ☆ ✿
Remove foliage to allow the flowers to develop

Thymus
Thyme (Herb)
Foliage (all year) Flowers (summer) ②③ ○ ☆

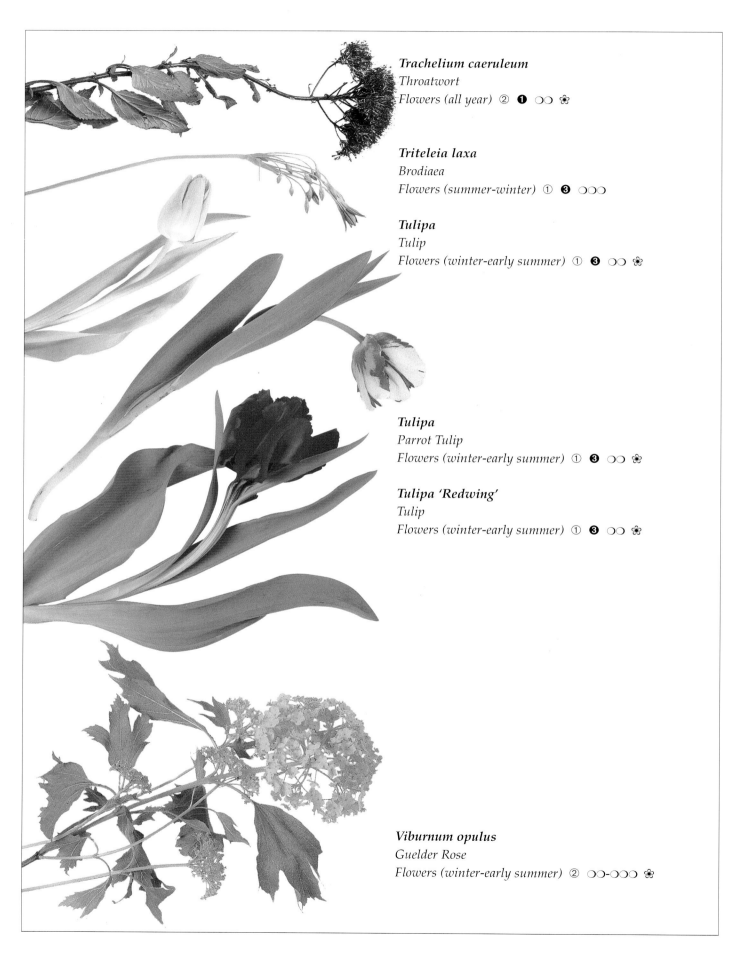

Trachelium caeruleum
Throatwort
Flowers (all year) ② ❶ ○○ ✿

Triteleia laxa
Brodiaea
Flowers (summer-winter) ① ❸ ○○○

Tulipa
Tulip
Flowers (winter-early summer) ① ❸ ○○ ✿

Tulipa
Parrot Tulip
Flowers (winter-early summer) ① ❸ ○○ ✿

Tulipa 'Redwing'
Tulip
Flowers (winter-early summer) ① ❸ ○○ ✿

Viburnum opulus
Guelder Rose
Flowers (winter-early summer) ② ○○-○○○ ✿

Viburnum tinus
Laurustinus
Foliage (all year) ❷ *Flowers (nealy all year)* ① ००○

Viburnum tinus
Laurustinus
Berries (autumn-winter) ① ००○

Viola
Viola
Flowers (summer) ③ ❸ ○ ✿

Weigela
Weigela
Foliage (spring-autumn) Flowers (summer)
② ❷ ○○ ✿

Zantedeschia
Arum – Calla Lily
Foliage and Flowers (all year) ① ❸ ००-००○ ✿

Zingiber officinale
Ginger
Flowers (intermittently) ① ००

INDEX

ACKNOWLEDGEMENTS

All photographs by Di Lewis (© Salamander Books) apart from the following:

pages 5, 17 top by Tim Sandall (© Salamander Books)

pages 31, 32-3, 106, 107, 122, 123 by Simon Butcher (© Salamander Books)

page 10 bottom right by Susie Edwards

The Colour Wheel on p15 was reproduced with the permission of the National Association of Flower Arrangement Societies (NAFAS) and is published by the organisation in a handy leaflet form. For anyone wanting to begin competitive work, it is an invaluable source of information to tuck into your toolbox, as are many of their publications on other aspects of flower arranging. They are available from NAFAS, 21 Denbigh Street, London SW1V 2HF, United Kingdom

The author and publisher would like to thank the following individuals who allowed the use of their homes for photography:

Richard Collins
May Beth and Barry Bruckman
Caroline and David Lawrence
Linda and Bryan Smith.

Also Alistair Cook at Lambeth Palace Gardens, and a multitude of wholesalers at New Covent Garden Market, in particular J. Ray Flowers, for the photographic space they provided.